OWNING POSSIBLE

REVIEW

WHAT DO YOU THINK OF THE BOOK SO FAR?

Thanks so much for purchasing this book! We'd love to hear about your experience thus far.

<u>We invite you to write a review on Amazon.</u>

To show our appreciation we will email you a free copy of the colorful Digital PDF version of "While Quarantined". An e-workbook for those looking to grow emotionally, mentally, and Spiritually.

You can get a sneak peek of the inside of the digital E-workbook at trillionsmall.com/singlewhilequarantined

WRITE A REVIEW STEPS

1. Write a review on Amazon. To write a review on Amazon simply locate your order and click "Write a Product Review"
2. If you did not purchase the book from Amazon you can still leave a review by simply finding the book on Amazon and scrolling to the very bottom of the product page and clicking "Write a Customer Review"
3. Once you write the review. Visit trillionsmall.com/reviews or scan the QR code below with the camera on your phone.
4. Fill out the online form.
5. All done! We will double-check that your review was posted to Amazon and we will then send you your gift via email.

Thank you again. May this book add value to your life.

OWNING POSSIBLE
Your Guide to Making the Impossible Possible!

Dr. Trillion Small

They Speak Publishing

Owning Possible

Your Guide to Making the Impossible Possible!

© 2018, 2019 by Trillion Small

All rights reserved. No part of this book may be reproduced or transmitted in any form or by any means, electronic or mechanical, including photocopying, recording, or by any information storage and retrieval system, without permission in writing from the copyright owner.

Published by They Speak Publishing, Dallas, Texas

All scripture is used from the New King James Version, © 1982 by Thomas Nelson, Inc. All rights reserved. Used by permission.

Exceptions are indicated by KJV, NIV, or MSG.

THE HOLY BIBLE, NEW INTERNATIONAL VERSION®, NIV® Copyright © 1973, 1978, 1984, 2011 by Biblica, Inc.® Used by permission. All rights reserved worldwide.

"Scripture taken from The Message. Copyright © 1993, 1994, 1995, 1996, 2000, 2001, 2002. Used by permission of NavPress Publishing Group."

The names, details, and circumstances may have been changed to protect the privacy of those mentioned in this publication.

Headshot by Kauwuane Burton

Printed in the United States of America

OTHER BOOKS BY TRILLION SMALL

She's Possible: Find Your Irresistible You

The Caged Free Heart: Letting Go of the Past that Incarcerates (2nd Edition)

Internal Navigator: Basic Steps to Get You from Point A to Point B in Your Life (2nd Edition)

I DEDICATE THIS BOOK TO THE FOLLOWING:

To God, the Master of the Impossible. Without Him, nothing is possible.

To the one who birthed and named me. A Trillion dollars doesn't seem as impossible now ☺

To all of my friends, family, and mentors who continue to challenge my thinking and push me beyond any limits.

To anyone who is ready to turn the impossible into the possible!

SCRIPTURE FOUNDATION FOR OWNING POSSIBLE

John 15:1-8

"I am the true vine, and My Father is the vinedresser. ² Every branch in Me that does not bear fruit He takes away; and every branch that bears fruit He prunes, that it may bear more fruit. ³ You are already clean because of the word which I have spoken to you. ⁴ Abide in Me, and I in you. As the branch cannot bear fruit of itself, unless it abides in the vine, neither can you, unless you abide in Me.

⁵ "I am the vine, you are the branches. He who abides in Me, and I in him, bears much fruit; for without Me you can do nothing. ⁶ If anyone does not abide in Me, he is cast out as a branch and is withered; and they gather them and throw them into the fire, and they are burned. ⁷ If you abide in Me, and My words abide in you, you will ask what you desire, and it shall be done for you. ⁸ By this My Father is glorified, that you bear much fruit; so you will be My disciples."

TABLE OF CONTENTS

Part 1- Prepare for the Mission

	Introduction- Mission Possible	17
1	You are Possible	27
2	Tools for the Possible	51

Part 2- Accept Your Mission

3	Move You Out of the Way	71
4	Perspective Matters	81
5	No Room for Fear	89
6	Speak Up and Ask	97
7	Don't Take No for an Answer	105
8	Walk on Faith	113
9	It Takes Vulnerability	123
10	You are Not in it Alone	133
11	Inconveniences are Your Best Friend	143
12	Develop Your Foresight	157
	Epilogue	171
	Chapter Notes	175

Part 1

PREPARE FOR THE MISSION

Here we will lay the foundation needed for your mission possible journey!

INTRODUCTION
MISSION POSSIBLE

One day I was driving listening to my Bible app. The narrator starts reading Mark 11 and my ears become more attentive to verse 22 that reads, *"²² So Jesus answered and said to them, "Have faith in God. ²³ For assuredly, I say to you, whoever says to this mountain, 'Be removed and be cast into the sea,' and does not doubt in his heart, but believes that those things he says will be done, he will have whatever he says."* It's getting good to me, so I nod in agreement as I anticipate hearing more. He reads on; " *²⁴ Therefore I say to you, whatever things you ask when you pray, believe that you receive them, and you will have them."* Wait. Pause. Rewind. He repeats it, " *²⁴ Therefore I say to you, whatever things you ask..."* I press pause so that I can have a quick discussion with God because at this point I am having a mind-blowing ah-ha moment! The conversation went something like this:

Me: Wait a minute God. Now, what exactly do you mean when you use the word *"whatever"* because, I mean, that is a pretty bold word to use here!

God: I mean *whatever*.

Me: Soo, like, *whatever?!*

God: *Yes, whatever.*

Me: Hmm, well what's the catch?

God: There is no catch. *Whatever* means *whatever*.

I have read this scripture so many times, but there was something special about hearing it that day! At that moment I received a glimpse into what it truly meant to live under an open Heaven and to have things manifest on Earth as they already are in Heaven[1].

My mind awoke on that day to a world full of possibilities. It was on that day that I realized,

NOTHING was impossible with God and WHATEVER I set out to do would be successful.

That is the purpose of this book. To serve as a notice that nothing is impossible with God and when you align yourself with the will of God, you can ask whatever and it will be done. The Gospel of John does not mention the above parable of the withered fig tree but in John 14:12-14 we do see a similar *whatever* declaration. Jesus says, *"Most assuredly, I say to you, he who believes in Me, the works that I do he will do also; and greater works than these he will do, because I go to My Father. [13] And whatever you ask in My name, that I will do, that the Father may be glorified in the Son. [14] If you ask anything in My name, I will do it."* There it is again, that *whatever* word. I love this scripture because it captures the true essence of what is needed to shift the impossible to possible. It is an intimate connection with God.

Now if you are looking to do the impossible solely by your strength then this book is not for you but if you realize that you cannot do it on your own then keep reading.

You may be thinking, "Trillion, we literally can't do ANYTHING we want," and I can see your side of the argument. My focus, however, is not to tell you all of the things you cannot do. My concentration in this book is to help you find and own what is possible for you, individually. That's what *Owning Possible* is all about! Discovering all of the impossible tasks that YOU were designed to make possible! The impossible becomes possible when you own it. Simply put, if you are not actively engaged (mentally, emotionally, spiritually, and physically) in possessing what could be yours then it will remain impossible.

So what is possible that you can own? We will soon discover that but keep in mind; your possible may not be your neighbor's possible. I will never be an astronaut, or a surgeon, or an engineer, or a NASCAR racecar driver, or an opera singer, or a WNBA player, or an Olympic swimmer. I know, never say never but at this point, I can assure you that I will never be any of these things. For one, I do not desire for God to make me all of these things, so I am not expending my faith on something that I don't even want. Plus, even if I did have the faith and the desire, I frankly do not have the capacity to do some of these things. Yes, I do believe in miracles so I could have an opera voice overnight, but until that happens, I will spend my time focusing on what I already have and focus on what I am created to do. So as you can see, owning your possible is a mixture of faith, capacity, and desire. I believe that if you have all three, you have the perfect recipe to make the impossible possible in your life.

I must warn you though. While reading this book your desires may change. What you once desired you may no longer want and what you never desired, may become a burning passion. Here is where it is important to ask God to help your desires submit to His will. Some of you all are still desiring and believing to marry Beyoncé or to have been

Prince Harry's princess. Well, they are both married so instead of wishing for their divorce, ask the Lord to make those desires submit to Him and redirect your focus. I'm just saying.

Scripture does remind us that He will give us the desires of our heart. Some take this to mean that whatever we want, He will do. I'd like to think it means that He plants our desires in our heart. Let me explain. I have heard that pregnant women can have weird cravings while pregnant; like a pop tart and a pickle…at the same time. #Gross. Her body can also reject food that she once could eat but no longer can, now that she is pregnant. So as you take this journey with me, honestly pay attention to your desires. Pay attention to your new cravings and pay attention to what is no longer appealing to you. It means you are pregnant with something and I can't wait to see what you manifest. That current man, or woman, or habit, or career may lose its appeal while that new man, or woman, or habit, or career may all of a sudden look more attractive. I believe your brand-new desires inside of you are an indicator of what may be possible for you. Don't worry about how impossible it may seem because w*hat is impossible for man is possible with God*[2].

So are you ready to get this mission possible journey started? I hope so. This journey will help you get the best use out of your unique design. Speaking of design, let's take a quick lesson from your kitchen drawer before moving on. Mrs. Fork is lovely and sparkly just like Mrs. Spoon, but Mrs. Fork will have a near impossible time eating chicken broth soup like Mrs. Spoon. Instead of being jealous of Mrs. Spoon, however, all Mrs. Fork has to do is focus on those things that she is good at such as picking up solid chicken, salad, and green beans. Now, if they both tried hard they could do each other's job, but we must admit that each is more effective in doing one thing over another.

The point is that we are all unique vessels crafted in God's hands and we all have a unique purpose to serve. We are all one body but made up of many members[3]. Thank goodness our feet chose to stay in their place and didn't try to become eyes! How would we walk? The same goes for you. Don't worry about what other people have and what they can do. We need YOU to play the role YOU were best created to play! We need you to step up, step out, and own your possible! This puzzle called society will forever miss a piece if you don't.

Reflection Questions

1. This journey will highlight both internal and external areas in your life that may seem impossible to obtain or overcome. Create a list of both internal and external areas in your life that you feel will be nearly impossible to happen (i.e., rekindling the love in your marriage, seeing your child receive salvation, getting that job you desire, forgiving your abuser, etc.)
2. Can you think of a time when you felt something would be impossible, but it turned out to be possible? Journal what the experience was.
3. Read I Corinthians 12 and journal about the insights that you receive while reading.

CHAPTER 1
YOU ARE POSSIBLE

A few years ago I was introduced to a poem called *Equipment* by Edgar Guest. I encourage you to search for it and read it as soon as you can. This poem confirmed to me that I already have every single thing I need to be successful and to own my possible. But I didn't always think that way. I use to think that I needed another degree, or another certification or another skill to finally be able to do what God had called me to do. Now, of course, some fields require a certain level of education and training, rightfully so, so don't drop this book and run to the hospital trying to doctor on somebody without going to medical school. We will visit you in prison. Just kidding. Not kidding.

To summarize, Mr. Guest's poem is telling you that you have all the equipment you need. You were born with it. Now, the most significant challenge is to overcome what you think about yourself and your perceived limitations. Once you surmount that hurdle, the next challenge is to figure out what in the world your message is and how you will demonstrate your possible to the world.

I'm sure you have seen the word impossible divided to then read I'm possible; I am possible. So your ability to make this shift from impossible to I'm possible relies on your ability to pull out who you are. I'm = I am. If God calls Himself *The Great I Am*[1] and if you were made in His image[2] then not only is He possible but so are you. Which then gives me all the more reason to boldly state that you are the person in which you have been looking. God is not giving you a message. Why? Because you ARE the message! You ARE the possible you have been seeking! It's right there inside of you! This thought reminds me of something God said to me as I was waking up on March 25, 2017. He whispered to my heart, "the best news you could give someone is you wrapped up in a newspaper." You, my friend, are the good news people need to read. Let your life be a story that people will read and leave inspired.

Your best work and your highest influence are going to come from whom you already are. Your greatest anointing flows in the areas that your past has prepared you. So don't just entirely do away with your history. Learn from it, heal from it, be encouraged by it, and impact the world with it. Your past experiences are just pieces of fabric beautifully woven together to make a beautiful and unique tapestry that tells a story that only you can narrate with justice. So own your story and tell your story. Someone needs to hear it. But of course, this requires you getting out of your comfort zone.

This is an Inside Job

The phrase "inside job" is used to describe an offense or crime that was done by somebody who already had access to confidential information.

Somebody who had close relationship with the person or organization did it. An example would be the manager of a bank helping his partner rob the bank at night. Now, of course, I am not asking you to commit a crime against yourself. The point I am trying to make is, who knows you better than you? Who is closest to you besides you (and Jesus)? Who knows your deep dark secrets better than you? Who spends every single waking and sleeping moment with you? You have the inside scoop on what is going on inside of you. Now I've never committed an inside job crime (or an outside job crime for that matter), but I'd assume the offense is much more possible when done with an inside person.

I'd like to propose that all of your external mission possibles will be so much easier when you have internally made up in your mind, without a shadow of a doubt, that what you desire is in fact, possible! Luke 6:45 says, "*A good man out of the good treasure of his heart brings forth good; and an evil man out of the evil treasure of his heart brings forth evil. For out of the abundance of the heart his mouth speaks."* This means your external manifestation is a direct reflection of your internal reality! Get your heart right, and everything else will follow suit. The greatest barrier to your mission possible is the condition of your heart. A cold, hard, and rigid heart absolutely will not reap the positive fruit that you seek to see. Ultimately, a changed heart begins with intimacy with the Father. The closer you are with Him, the more in tune you are with Him, and I'd like to think the more He desires to bless and show you favor. A sincere and grateful heart just makes people want to continue to do for you.

Get Out of the Box

I am not a huge automobile fan, but I do have a thing for large SUVs, so I have been considering trading in my small SUV for a larger one. I was talking to my brother about the different options I was looking at, and I remember telling him, "man I am sure going to miss squeezing into those compact car parking spaces!" This was so ironic because I was concerned about being too big to park close, out of all the other things that should be more concerning! I wasn't worried about the increase in gas I'd be paying or how I'd have to drive much slower than my heavy foot would like. No, I was concerned about where I was going to be able to park the huge thing! And then it dawned on me, small is so convenient!

I wonder how many of us are actually like this in our personal, relational, and professional life. We realize that we deserve more and we have the opportunity to have more yet we settle for small because it is convenient. How many red flags did it take for you to realize that he or she was no good for you? How many times will you go home with your wig half off because your work environment is merely driving you up the wall giving you every indication that it is time to transition? How many social gatherings or networking events are you going to turn down before you realize you will not and cannot grow personally or professionally in your little shell?

Being I'm-Possible will, without a shadow of a doubt, require you to step out of your shell, out of your bubble, and out of the box. Whichever one you have been hiding in. Which then means you must be comfortable with being uncomfortable until the uncomfortable is no longer uncomfortable for you (or at least more bearable). Yes, I know that nobody likes to make themselves intentionally feel uncomfortable but just like weight training; without the resistance and the tearing of your muscles, you won't get any bigger. If we always play it small and safe, we will never max out on our full potential.

So what is it that makes us want to stay so small? I believe one of my dreams on May 20, 2017, gave me the perfect answer and illustration. *Side note first: If you aren't already, I encourage you to begin writing down all of your dreams, visions, and ah-ha moments in a journal or your note section on your phone. They are invaluable stories and lessons that you may want to share one day, just as I've done all throughout this book.* Ok so back to the dream. I was flying my helicopter, but I was flying very low as if I was a car. I was more familiar with driving cars, so this whole helicopter thing was new to me. I could tell I was new because I was struggling a little to fly it smoothly. This new adventure was so fun yet so scary, and that is why I decided to fly so low. I figured if I fly low with the cars I wouldn't have a far way to crash if I were to. I wanted to stay low and small because I was afraid. I woke from this dream and wrote, "As my mind elevates so will my actions."

Do you have high-flying potential but still settle for a low car driving mentality? What is causing you to be so afraid? Failure? Rejection? Losing? I can guarantee you that if you elevated your perspective those things wouldn't seem as daunting as you think them to be. It appears that David understood this principle when he wrote in Psalm 119:71, *"It was good for me that I was afflicted, that I may learn your statues."*

Instead of looking at failure, rejections, and losses as negatives, look at them as indicators that you are trying, growing, and learning! You can't fail if you never sign up for the race, you can't be rejected if you never put yourself out there to be chosen, and you can't lose in a game that you never entered. That's the good news.

The bad news is that you also cannot succeed, or be chosen, or win if you don't do these things either! So what's it going to take for you to get out of the box? You must elevate your mind. Elevate your thinking to a level that sees no limits, knows no barriers, and refuses to settle!

God gave me a beautiful lesson on settling while I was discussing an ex with Him. I was telling God how I was thinking of trying again with a guy I once dated who was trying to rekindle a relationship with me. Very clearly God told me that if I went back to him not only would I be settling but I would be sub-settling. Now I knew what settling was, but I had no idea what sub-settling was. It's not even an actual word, but hey He is God so He can make up words if He wishes. He went on to explain sub-settling by using a building illustration. So imagine that what God has promised you is the size of a 3-story building. You would be settling if you just took the 2-story house and you would be sub-settling if you just took the one bedroom loft. So basically, sub-settling is settling for what was already beneath what God had promised for you! Now that's low!

Of course, I didn't go back to the guy, but settling can look so appealing at the time, particularly when presented with just a crumb of what your heart desires. But you must ask yourself, will I settle for this crumb or will I wait to own the restaurant? Will I settle for Ishmael or will I wait for Isaac[3] ?

People, places, and things will try to keep you in your box and persuade you to settle, and your heart may do more convincing than these. One, because it's our natural tendency to play it safe for survival purposes and it's the enemies way of causing you to abort God's full promises for your life. And two, if you step out of your box you then challenge other people's comfort zone. I don't know if you have every challenged someone else's comfort zone who was contented with complacency but oh boy do they NOT like it! But that is none of your concern. You will be just fine if you fight to overcome your barriers and don't worry yourself about making other people comfortable. It's not your job to sooth their insecurities. So don't fly low to appease someone who is afraid of heights! You must take ownership of your own life and be intentional daily about choosing to dream big and fly high. The possible has no room for mediocre, normal, and average folk and I believe Maya Angelou said it best. *"If you are always trying to be normal, you will never know how amazing you can be."*

Make a Choice to be I'm-Possible

Getting out of the box requires that you make choices. You will need to make a cognitive choice, a verbal choice, and an action choice. It's not just a 100% mental choice. You must actively play your role in your story. Some would say if you believe it then it's yours but you can sit in your closet all day praying for a hot dog, but if you don't get out of the closet to a location that has hot dogs then you won't get one. If you and your husband believe to have a baby then you both probably should be having sex; right? Seems like a no-brainer but some people fail to realize that they still have a part to play. I once heard Bishop T.D. Jakes say that God doesn't make tables; He makes trees so stop waiting on God to do what you can do. You do your part and let God do the rest.

How many times have you said, "I'm waiting on God to do it (whatever that IT was)?" or "I will pray about it and wait for more confirmation before I make a move?" I am guilty of both, and I have found that although they sound "theologically proper" there are times when this is not spiritually sound.

We had a guest speaker come to the church I attended back in Nashville, TN and he asked the question, "how many times have we said, 'I am waiting on God to show me where to go before I move.' But God is saying, 'I will tell you where to go WHEN you move!'"

Another pastor said it very plain and simple, "many times we think we are waiting on God but in actuality, He is waiting for us!"

We try to use these things to justify our "faith" and "trust" in God, but if you ask me, these are just excuses to cover up your fear, doubt, or complacency. I believe that so many of us will never reach our fullest potential because we are "waiting for more confirmation." Not saying that God will not confirm what He has told you, because He will, and I am not saying that you should not seek Him in the decisions you are trying to make, because you should, but many times we ALREADY know what we should do but remain stagnant and stuck by fear or some other third variable.

I say all of this to reemphasize my point. You have a part and a role to play in this relationship too. If you want a job, then fill out applications rather than sit at home as if it will walk to you. If you want to receive, then give. If you are looking for Mr. or Mrs. Right and it is your time then get out and mingle; unless you think God will UPS him/her to you. You do what you can and then let God fulfill His part. Don't try to do His part and don't try to short-cut on your part. Fulfill all that you can, and God will take it from there. It may be in our nature, but I think we make things so complicated when it really is not that difficult. Do your part, and He will do His! Plain and simple.

Yes, the woman with the issue of blood was healed by her faith, but it was her crawling to Jesus to touch the hem of His garment that matched her faith to make it reality[4]. I call this positioning yourself for what you believe! If the wide receiver is believing and hoping to make a touch down then he sure better be certain to first position himself to catch the ball! Nobody has ever made a touchdown by sitting on the bench! Get in the game of life! You are the lead role in YOUR show so show up for it every single day!

Think, Speak, and Act Your Way to Possible

Everything that you have ever seen manifest on the outside at one point began on the inside; from the inside of a person's heart, mind, and spirit. Every creation of the Earth started with an idea from God that He then spoke into existence and every witty invention made my man's hand started the same way. It all began as an idea, that when coupled with words and an action plan, turned into reality. That's right; our thoughts have the power to create the world we want.

So, allow your words and your actions to line up with what you believe and what you see in your mind's eye as you prepare yourself to own your possible. The woman with the issue of blood kept saying to herself, *"If only I may touch His garment, I shall be made well."*[5] She's speaking and crawling, crawling and speaking. Her belief was backed by what she was willing to do to get it.

I don't know if you noticed, but in this story, Jesus was moving on and heading to raise a girl from the dead. This crawling woman with an issue technically wasn't on His agenda for the day. He wasn't about to stop and turn around so that she could touch Him. That wasn't His part. That was her part. She put herself on His agenda with her actions.

If the woman with the issue of blood were to go into her impossible situation with an "I can't," "this is too hard," "this will be impossible" mindset then she would have set herself up automatically to fail. Henry Ford once said, *"Whether you think you can, or you think you can't – you're right."* So wisely choose what you think and wisely choose what you speak. Why? Because what you think, you will speak, and what you speak, you will do and become. Your weapon is in your mouth. Your tongue is the key that holds your possible. Either your mouth will lock you out of what is already yours, or it will give you full access to the promises of your life.

Not only do you need to be mindful of your words, but it is also vital that you are also cognizant of your thoughts. Going into a seemingly impossible situation with a negative or divided mindset is like starting a long road trip with your gas tank on empty. You may start, but you won't go far at all. It's like attempting to take an uphill journey but insisting on walking downhill. A divided mind not only will confuse the manifestation but it will also stall the process.

Be as selective in what you mentally sow as a gardener. They know in advance if they want to reap apples or oranges and they sow accordingly! They don't just throw one hundred seeds down a hole and hope for the best. Let's learn from them. What do you want? Do you want to win or not? Do you want your promises or not? Being confused in what you want is like coming to a fork in the road and deciding to turn right, but as soon as you turn the wheel, you change your mind and choose to go left, and as soon as you turn left you back up and choose to go right again. Ultimately, you are going nowhere fast. So make a CHOICE and stick with it. Need I remind you that YES, you do have a choice and your possible is depending on you to make a wise one!

There are Possibilities Galore

Possibilities. Possibilities. Possibilities. There are endless possibilities all around. When you think about it, there are endless negative possibilities, and there are endless positive possibilities. But the good thing is you can choose which you will focus. I recall telling this guy I just met about an awesome woman that I met and how excited I was to collaborate with her and support her organization as she helped support me in my entrepreneur endeavors. After expressing my joy, he asks me, "What would you do if this lady betrays you?" I was completely thrown off by such a misplaced question.

Truthfully I didn't even entertain the question because I didn't want to begin feeding my mind with unnecessary fear and doubt that came from my imagination. I kindly but firmly told this guy how I felt about his silly question and I proceeded to tell him not to speak to me again. Now, this may seem like a super harsh punishment for a seemingly harmless question but I know the power of my thoughts, and I guard it and protect it at all costs. I have to be much more diligent and vigilant in guarding my mind especially since I know it tends to want to wander off course from time to time. I did what I felt was best for my mind and that was to eliminate any toxicity that wanted to creep in. I knew even entertaining the simple question would bear zero positive fruit, so I chose not to focus on it.

Just like me, all kinds of possibilities will arise but you can choose which ones you will entertain, and you can choose which ones to cut off. And as you are choosing, be mindful of II Corinthians 10:5 (KJV) that says, "*Casting down imaginations, and every high thing that exalteth itself against the knowledge of God, and bringing into captivity every thought to the obedience of Christ.*" Now yes, when you are strategizing for the future of your company or team you do have to take into consideration the pros and cons as well as the possible hurdles ahead so that you can plan accordingly, but you don't have to dwell on everything that could go wrong, because it probably will if you expend so much energy focusing on it. Spend more time focusing on what you do want and less time focusing on what you don't want.

For example, instead of saying, "I don't want to lose my current customers" try saying, " I want to do what it takes to keep my customers satisfied." Or, instead of saying, "I don't like when you ____ [to your spouse/child/employee]" try saying, I like it when you_____." Do you hear the difference? The first one focuses on the negatives, and the latter encourages production of more of what you want to see.

So let's see what all is possible. Go to the next page, and I will show you how an unlimited amount of possibilities look…

Wait, did you see it? I think you moved past it too quickly. Look back one page and look again. You may be thinking, "it was nothing but a blank page," but oh I beg to differ! It was a page full of endless possibilities that you can create! Stare at that page until you can dream and imagine far beyond your reach!

Reflection Questions

1. What is holding you back from owning your message and stepping out of the box?
2. Which choice do you wrestle with the most? Making a mental, verbal, or action choice? Write it down and talk about what makes it so challenging for you.
3. When you stared at that blank page what concepts, ideas, and plans came to mind? If nothing, then go back and stare at it again until your creative mind begins to flow.

CHAPTER 2
TOOLS FOR THE POSSIBLE

In chapter one we discussed how you already have all of the equipment that you need to make the impossible possible. So metaphorically speaking, you are the car, but now we need the fuel, which is what will give you the energy and power to make forward movement.

Faith

In Matthew 14 we find Peter doing what no other man has ever done, and that is walking on water. He was walking on water, but it was his faith that sustained his feet because the moment he begins to sink the Lord questions his faith. It was his faith that allowed him to do the impossible. What's interesting though, is that when we read this story, we rarely marvel at the fact that Jesus is also walking on water. We mainly focus on Peter doing it. But why? Yes, Jesus was God wrapped in the flesh, but He was both divine and human.

We are given all throughout scripture the opportunity to witness how the human part of Him had limits without God's help. He even says so in John 5:19-20. *"Then Jesus answered and said to them, "Most assuredly, I say to you, the Son can do nothing of Himself, but what He sees the Father do; for whatever He does, the Son also does in like manner. [20] For the Father loves the Son, and shows Him all things that He Himself does; and He will show Him greater works than these, that you may marvel."*

We should marvel just as much about Jesus walking on water as we do Peter because based on the above scripture, walking on water wouldn't have even been possible if it wasn't for God. Jesus could walk on water because He kept His eyes on God and mimicked what was possible. Peter also could walk on water because he had his eyes on Jesus. It wasn't until he took his eyes off Jesus that he began to sink.

Shifting the impossible to possible only works when you fully focus on the Lord. As you gaze upon Him and discover what He is doing, you will be able to mimic it. The moment you begin to feel yourself sinking, ask yourself, "Where are my eyes?" You will be able to do nothing of yourself but what you see Him do.

Focus

I recall a time when a friend and I were at Dave & Buster's. I was sitting back watching him play Pac-Man on this jumbo screen and in the middle of the game this little toddler about two years old walks right in front of the screen. He was so tiny so he didn't cover the entire screen but his little head did cover the bottom screen. The child didn't seem to break his concentration, so I asked if he had just seen that child walk across the bottom of the screen and he was like "what child?" That's the kind of focus you need. The kind that causes you to zoom in on what's important and eliminate all distractions! I want you to be so focused that you don't even notice the negative possibilities.

When you make your priorities your focus and not your parameters you can have a clear focus. The moment you feel off balance, unclear, and uncertain ask yourself if you have lost your focus. If you are a visionary or an entrepreneur, then you may have experienced scattered attention a time or two. I know the feeling. You have a million and one fantastic ideas that you want to start but because your focus is so divided, you never really get the chance to make that one or two things excellent.

Write down all that you are doing and all that you desire to do. Now out of all of those things, which one or two things will allow you to reap the most from the time and energy that you invest in it? Start with that idea, and then expand from there, but whatever the project or goal is, focus, focus, focus.

If the enemy can distract you, he can delay the process. This season is NOT the time to be distracted. Find your focal point and focus! This is the time where you will have to say NO more than you say YES.

A Vested Interest

I practice mental health counseling, and one of the things I often tell my clients early on is that I will work hard and fight with you in your healing journey but what I will not do is work harder than you are willing to work for yourself. I rarely saw optimal results when I was the one doing all of the heavy lifting. I will support and spot you as you lift your heavyweight, but I will not lift it for you.

What I am assessing for when I say this is just how much the client is willing to invest in him or herself to see the change they desire. One of my favorite leadership mentors, John Maxwell, said, "People who achieve their potential do so because they invest in themselves every day." Are you truly committed to what you believe? If so, where is your proof? Show me your skin in the game. You say you want to drop 50 pounds so show me your gym membership, fitness trainer, nutritionist, or healthy cookbooks. You say you want to gross a million dollars this year so show me your network, business strategy, or your personal "clocked hours" of diligent work. You say you want to write a book, become a professional singer, become a professional speaker, become a _____, so show me your proof that this is in fact what you want? Where are the word documents, videos, workshops, etc. to prove it?

Throw yourself 100% into whatever you have set out to accomplish. Have a real vested interest or move aside for those who are serious about it. Martin Luther King, Jr. said it best in one of his sermons titled, "The Three Dimensions of a Complete Life[1] ":

What I'm saying to you this morning, my friends, even if it falls your lot to be a street sweeper, go on out and sweep streets like Michelangelo painted pictures; sweep streets like Handel and Beethoven composed music; sweep streets like Shakespeare wrote poetry; sweep streets so well that all the host of heaven and earth will have to pause and say,

'Here lived a great street sweeper who swept his job well.'

If you can't be a pine on the top of a hill
Be a scrub in the valley—but be
The best little scrub on the side of the hill,
Be a bush if you can't be a tree.
If you can't be a highway just be a trail
If you can't be the sun be a star;
It isn't by size that you win or fail-
Be the best of whatever you are."

This message is not a suggestion to settle. It is instead a commission to own whatever is YOUR possible and be the best at it!

A Spirit of Excellence

If you do not wish to do your best and be your best and you are content with a "that'll do" attitude, why are you even doing it? I Corinthians 10:31 states, *"Therefore, whether you eat or drink, or whatever you do, do all to the glory of God."*

I remember turning in an application to an organization that I wanted to join. The young lady took one look at my application and without even reading the content, said, "wow, now this is what we call done in excellence." I didn't just turn in the application stapled together. No, I printed it in color on nice paper, added a headshot, resume, and a short bio, and I put it in a bound folder. I even made a cover page, a title page, and a table of contents page for it with the pages numbered. All in which they didn't ask of me. They just wanted my answers to their questions. Maybe that is just the writer in me, but I knew even the presentation of my application would speak for me and I wanted it to say that I was not mediocre and that I would go above and beyond what is asked of me to get the job done.

Speaking of presentation; even your appearance speaks for you so what is it saying? I recall being at a networking breakfast in which I was probably the only millennial surrounded by a room of baby boomers. I loved it. I don't shy away from great opportunities to connect with generations before me!

That is how I learn and grow. So, after the speaker concluded, a gentleman at my table and I began to have a conversation. We talked about many things including appearance. He asked who taught me how to be so well dressed and poised. Of course, I had to give kudos to my mom because she teaches us about being mindful of what we wear and how we look when we leave the house. He seemed to be very impressed and stated that I have what he likes to call executive presence. Now, that was such a pleasant compliment. He even made that statement, not because of the words that came out of my mouth, but because of the statement of excellence that I made from my appearance. To this day he is still so gracious to continuously invite me to networking events and social gatherings that will help me to connect with other awesome people in the city.

I don't share these things to brag or to impress you but to impress upon you that your greatest victories and breakthroughs will not solely come from the works of your hands. A great deal of it will come when people see that you walk in a spirit of excellence, dignity, respect, and character. That is a person you can trust. Of course, favor and the person liking you are obviously key factors as well. I don't know about you, but when I see that a person operates with integrity and excellence, I am more likely to like them and as a result, I will want to help them.

Confidence

I believe one of the core elements of having an executive presence is confidence. It's a certain air that you give off when you walk in the room that just naturally draws people to your side of the room to talk with you. It's that warm and welcome invitation that your presence alone brings.

I asked a few women what their greatest barriers were to going out to networking events, and each said that they were shy. Me not being satisfied with that answer probed more to find out what "shy" meant to her. I'm not shy, so I really did want to understand it. I finally found the root after we dug deeper. Being shy actually translated to mean, "I don't have the confidence to do that." Some even called themselves introverts, and we actually ended up at the same root problem. Low confidence.

In my networking and socializing experience, I have observed that the most confident people are the ones who know who they are and they believe they add value to the room. One young lady shared that she didn't like to network with people who were at a higher level than her career-wise and financially. I tried explaining that those are actually the best type of networking events. You always want to surround yourself with people who are further ahead than you are on the journey so that you can continue to grow and develop. Who will challenge whom to become more if everybody was on the same playing field? Yes, put me in a room full of millionaires and billionaires! My goal is to become a trillionaire (☺), so I need to learn how to accumulate great wealth. I love thousandaires too, but I really want to learn from those who have been there and done that and have the bank statements to show for it.

What I am trying to say is this, low confidence will keep you out of rooms that you need to be in and will keep you away from tables where you should be sitting. Confidence is sexy, and I don't mean that sensually, but it truly makes you a magnet. It is super attractive, and people like to be around it. If they don't, then they may be insecure. When you walk in the room, own it.

When you walk in that meeting, own it. Hold your head up, stick your chest out, and look like you belong in the room. That final key that you need to unlock your possible may be in that room, so work it.

Understand Timing and the Process

I moved to Dallas, Texas on July 5, 2017. God confirmed in March 2017 that He, in fact, wanted me to move from Nashville, Tennessee. It wasn't the first time He spoke to me about Dallas, however. I recall Him also talking to me in 2015 about moving to Dallas. I even began the moving process by flying to Dallas to look for an apartment. No matter what, however, I didn't have full peace about my decision back in 2015, so I delayed the move. The idea of moving came back up in 2017, and this time I had 100% peace with it once He confirmed and I had an intense sense of urgency to move.

That desire back in 2015 wasn't wrong. It was right, but the timing wasn't. In 2017 I realized that I simply wasn't ready back in 2015 and I would have squandered every opportunity and relationship that He is giving me now had He presented it to me back then. It took me several years to finally realize that just because God gives me a vision or a dream today, doesn't mean He is going to make it happen right away. Usually, the dream is a friendly indicator that a process to develop will soon follow.

Everyone's process may look different, but I do know that two of the classes in the process is character development and habit shifting. Maybe God needs time to teach you humility or to teach you how to forgive or to teach you how to let go of control. And then perhaps He is giving you time to earn your degree or finish that certification program. Whatever your process looks like, trust that God is intentional and purposeful in every step that He has you to take.

I use to have such a difficult time with God's timing especially if His timing didn't quite line up with my "I want it right now" kind of attitude. But God has been so patient in teaching me how to appreciate His timing. I still haven't mastered it, but I am so much better than I was before. Maybe you can relate, but I have been holding on to so many dreams for many years. There were times when I felt disappointed and hopeless and felt that it would just be best not to hope because at least then I wouldn't get my hopes up AGAIN! But it wasn't until I stepped foot on Dallas ground as a resident that I began to see each dream unfold so beautifully and quickly. Things that He told me seven years ago are just now breaking ground. I'm glad I didn't give up on those dreams just because they didn't happen instantaneously. When you finally see the fruit of the seeds that were planted you forget about all the pain and agony that waiting may have put you through. Sort of like having a baby, so I have been told. All of the excruciating pain is gone when you look into the eyes of your brand new miracle.

Just like birthing a baby, it doesn't happen overnight! The baby needs time to develop. No mentally sane mother wants to have a premature baby! No matter how uncomfortable her pregnancy is, she wants to birth a healthy baby, so she is willing to endure until the end to be sure that happens. So why do we find ourselves wanting to rush and terminate the process before it is time? I finally found a fix for that. One day I was listening to my Bible in The Message (MSG) translation and Romans 8:22-25 just blessed my socks off and gave me a whole new perspective on waiting.

"All around us we observe a pregnant creation. The difficult times of pain throughout the world are simply birth pangs. But it's not only around us; it's within us. The Spirit of God is arousing us within. We're also feeling the birth pangs. These sterile and barren bodies of ours are yearning for full

deliverance. That is why waiting does not diminish us, any more than waiting diminishes a pregnant mother. We are enlarged in the waiting. We, of course, don't see what is enlarging us. But the longer we wait, the larger we become, and the more joyful our expectancy."

The wait doesn't diminish us, although it feels like it at times. The wait increases our capacity to hold what He is about to birth in us! I don't know about you, but that encourages me to hold on just a little while longer!

But if that still doesn't help, just think about Joseph's long and agonizing process in Genesis 27. There was about a 22-year gap between the time he had a dream about his destiny and the time of fulfillment. His entire journey had its ups and its downs. Each down seemed like he was moving further and further away from his dream but he wasn't. It was his downs that actually brought him closer to his dream. So if you ever begin to feel discouraged or impatient in your process, remember Habakkuk 2:3, *"For the vision is yet for an appointed time; but at the end it will speak, and it will not lie. Though it tarries, wait for it; because it will surely come, it will not tarry."* Believe that God will complete what He started in you[2]. Trust me, your patience will be tested during your mission, but endure the process and trust God's timing, trust His delays, and trust that He knows what He is doing. Even when you don't see His work with your own two eyes, know that He is still working behind the scenes on your behalf. Simply do your part and let Him worry about the rest.

Reflection Questions

1. What proof do you have to show that you are truly invested in the fulfillment of your purpose here on Earth?
2. Ponder on the other mission possible ingredients; faith, a spirit of excellence, confidence, focus, and understanding timing and the process. Which of these do you believe you have room to grow? Talk about why you think so.
3. What has God promised you that you are still waiting on? Write them all down; even the ones that you may have given up in believing.

Part 2

ACCEPT YOUR MISSION

In this section I have shared personal stories of both internal and external missions that challenged my limits and equipped me to own my possible. As you read these stories, you will naturally feed on the information that is most pertinent to your personal life.

What we do with our own experiences will determine when, where, and how we possess what is ours. Sometimes the internal missions seem more difficult, in particular, but we must endure through them. It is the overcoming of those internal struggles that then give us the freedom and flexibility to be the most effective externally. We are then able to tackle those external "impossibilities" with more zeal, power, and might.

CHAPTER 3
MOVE YOU OUT OF THE WAY

It was a long day at work, and I really wanted to go home and relax. However, upon examining my filthy car, I figured it was time for a car wash. That wasn't a bad idea, however, because washing my car was quite therapeutic for me and I really needed to clear my mind. So I get to the self-serve car wash port that they had in my apartment, and I pull in next to this older gentleman that was in his forties. My army fatigue shirt caught his eye because it read, "I Am On a Mission." He asked what my mission was and I replied sort of cliché'ish, "I am on a mission to fulfill God's commission." As soon as I said it, I thought to myself, "uh oh that means at some point during this car wash God is going to have me to say something to this man about Him."

So anyway, this man tries to continue small talk such as work, sports, etc. I engage him in conversation, but I really was not in the mood to talk to anyone at that time. Right as I am finishing up, God begins to speak. At first, I tried to brush it to the side because I really did not want to have to say something to him. I just wanted to wash my car and go home, but while I was cleaning my tires and rims off God kept nudging me. He then finally says something that made me pay attention. He said, "Are you going to be that selfish?" Feeling super convicted, I humbly replied, "No." I then asked the Lord what He wanted to tell me about this man. God tells me that this man's favorite hobby is golf, but he has been unable to play because of a back injury.

During this time in my life, God seemed to put me around people with back issues, and because of that, I began to wonder if it was just all in my head or if this man really had a back issue. I wasn't looking at the man much, but I did not notice him having back problems; I mean after all he was out there washing his car. I decide to walk over to the other side of my car where he was standing, and I began to ask him what he now does as far as hobbies go since he is retired. He told me he had to retire because of a back injury. As you could imagine, he now has ALL of my attention. He goes on to share that he had degenerative disc disease so he couldn't do much of anything besides go to the pool daily, sit on a float, and read. He said he actually shouldn't have even been washing his car because he'd be in great pain later. Gotta love God's positioning.

At this point, I have kicked into my "faith-time to heal mode." I begin talking about this other time when I prayed for a man who had a few herniated discs in his lower back. I shared this testimony as a faith builder and as a means to use a testimony as prophecy so that he could receive that same healing for himself if he desired and believed, *for the testimony of Jesus is the spirit of prophecy[1]."* He is kneeling down by his tires as I am saying this but he immediately jumps up and says, "Uh oh now, don't tell me this man got healed! You are gonna have to pray for me now!" I laugh, and I go on to tell him how the man indeed did get healed. He jumps with excitement and comes to the other side of his car where I was standing, and he throws his shirt up and points to the scar on his back and says, "Come on, lay hands on me!" This is funny because as he says it, a couple walks by and laughs as he shouts to them, "She is about to lay hands and heal me!"

This man's faith and excitement got me all the more excited! So I pray for his healing and afterward he turned and gave me a big hug and told me that I was a special person. I shared with him how I wasn't even planning on washing my car, and he said, "See God knew that somebody down here was going to need you." This man's overwhelming joy uplifted my spirits and made me forget about all of my "problems." This man needed something from God and God wanted to use me to give it to him, but for a second I was going to allow something so small to stop me from being used. I was about to be so selfish just because I felt that it was an inconvenient time for me.

But isn't it just like God? To use us in our brokenness to minister to those who are broken as well? While I am complaining about being tired while cleaning my tires God is trying to get me to see the bigger picture. When we are low, we feel that we have nothing to offer, but I want to encourage you to look for God's hand during those times because He can move in a super mighty way. When you are at your lowest, He is at His highest! Remove yourself, your selfish tendencies, your narrowed earthly perspective, and look at life from Heaven down to Earth.

Take every opportunity that you have. He may want you to say something to that stranger that you really do not feel like being bothered with but what if your words could save their life? Your sacrifice could result in joy for them, peace for them, healing for them, and even salvation for them. Even when you are tired and bent over trying to clean up your own dirty mess, take a step back and see those around you. Do you have what they need? If so, are you going to withhold what they need to make their mission possible?

Mission Possible

What did it take for this mission to be accomplished? Take some time to read each prayer and scripture below. Here are a few things it took:

- <u>A listening heart</u>- Lord, open my spiritual eyes and ears that I may be able to see and hear the things that you are speaking to me. Make me more sensitive to your voice.
  - *"But blessed are your eyes for they see, and your ears for they hear; ^{17} for assuredly, I say to you that many prophets and righteous men desired to see what you see, and did not see it, and to hear what you hear, and did not hear it." – Matthew 13:16-17*

- <u>A non-resistant heart</u>- Lord, I understand that when I resist your plan, it is symbolic of a dam in a river. I do not desire to be the barrier to the flow of your Spirit so please reveal to me the root of my resistance and help my heart yield to You.

- *"...throw away the foreign gods that are among you and yield your hearts to the Lord, the God of Israel." – Joshua 24:23 (NIV)*

- <u>Selflessness/humility</u>- Lord, give me a servants heart that I may be able to place your people above my selfish ambitions. Help me to see the value in them that You see.

- *"Do nothing out of selfish ambition or vain conceit. Rather, in humility value others above yourselves, [4] not looking to your own interests but each of you to the interests of the others." – Philippians 2:3-4*

- <u>Obedience</u>- Lord, help me to obey your voice so that all may be well between You and me.

- *"But this is what I commanded them, saying, 'Obey My voice, and I will be your God, and you shall be My people. And walk in all the ways that I have commanded you, that it may be well with you." – Jeremiah 7:23*

- What else did it take?

Reflection Questions

1. Think about a time you recall God speaking to you about another person's situation. How did you handle the information He entrusted to you?
2. Think about a time when you felt low, but someone also needed your encouragement. How did you handle a situation like that?
3. Sometimes selfishness can get the best of us all. What does it take for a person to be able to stop focusing so much on themselves and focus more on the needs of others?

CHAPTER 4
PERSPECTIVE MATTERS

I was on an airplane heading to who knows where at the time. All I recall is feeling ecstatic and antsy to get off the plane! The sun was shining, and from my point of view, it was going to be a lovely day when we landed. However, that was not the case! The pilot came over the intercom telling us that he had to delay landing just for a moment to allow the lightning to stop before we landed. I thought in my head, "uhm sir, what lighting? It is bright and shiny outside!" Lo and behold, when we finally broke through the clouds and were now beneath the clouds I was able to see what the pilot was saying. It wasn't sunny after all on the ground it was dark and rainy.

This immediately altered my happy go lucky mood to be a bit somber. Was I disillusioned by what I saw? I mean it was just clear and sunny a few minutes ago. No, I wasn't delusional. What I saw all depended on the altitude at which my perspective was. When I was high and above the dark clouds, I felt optimistic and hopeful about what was to come, but when I leveled with and below the dark clouds, I immediately had a mood shift.

Get Your Head Above the Clouds

I'm sure you have heard the saying, "get your head out of the clouds!" Typically, this is about someone who is daydreaming or not paying attention to his or her current surroundings, but I have come to tell you to keep your head ABOVE the clouds! Why? Because the higher you are, the less dreary your circumstances will appear and the higher you are, your perspective has to change. You will no longer look at your circumstances from Earth-up, but you will look at them the way that you are supposed to, and that is Heaven-down.

An Earth to Heaven perspective keeps you engulfed by all that is around you; so much so that it is difficult to see the sun (Son) on the other side of your trials. It is focusing on all the chaos and troubles and not seeing a way out. It is seeing all the doom and gloom without sight of a brighter day. A Heaven to Earth perspective is seeing things the way God does. It is seeing the ultimate end result and being full of hope, love, faith, and optimism despite what is going on.

Have you ever seen that commercial about depression with the little sad, dark cloud following the lady? What if the cloud isn't the problem? With my new ah-ha moment from the plane, I'd like to propose that it is more so about the positioning of your head in relation to the cloud. If the cloud is hovering over your head, of course, all you will see is darkness, but if you were to lift your head up above the clouds, you'd see that the sun was shining the entire time.

So I challenge you to look above the clouds of your life, look above the dark and gloomy news, look above the despair and dreadful circumstances and see the SON. The closer you get to Him the better He makes you and your life look. Don't fear what is around you but instead, choose to go up to another level and view your life and your circumstances the way Jesus does which is Heaven down to Earth and not Earth up to Heaven…it looks a lot better that way anyways.

Mission Possible Glasses

I will leave you with this beautiful prayer from Paul in Ephesians 1:16-21:

> *"[I] do not cease to give thanks for you, making mention of you in my prayers: [17] that the God of our Lord Jesus Christ, the Father of glory, may give to you the spirit of wisdom and revelation in the knowledge of Him, [18] the eyes of your understanding being*

enlightened; that you may know what is the hope of His calling, what are the riches of the glory of His inheritance in the saints, [19] and what is the exceeding greatness of His power toward us who believe, according to the working of His mighty power [20] which He worked in Christ when He raised Him from the dead and seated Him at His right hand in the heavenly places, [21] far above all principality and power and might and dominion, and every name that is named, not only in this age but also in that which is to come."

What you see and what you understand will make all the difference when it comes to seeing past the impossible. Your natural eyeglasses won't help you to see God's big vision for your life. Only your mission possible glasses can see something that big!

Mission Possible

What did it take for this mission to be accomplished? Take some time to read the prayer and scriptures below.

Here is one thing it took:

- <u>A change in perspective</u>- Lord, help me to see my life from Your perspective. I know that when I do, what seems like a big deal now, will no longer be as big as I thought it was. Elevate my mind and help me to see the bigger picture.
  - *" [He] raised us up together, and made us sit together in the heavenly places in Christ Jesus, [7] that in the ages to come He might show the exceeding riches of His grace in His kindness toward us in Christ Jesus." – Ephesians 2: 6-7*
  - *"The Lord said to my Lord, "Sit at My right hand, till I make Your enemies Your footstool." – Psalm 110:1*
- What else did it take?

Reflection Questions

1. As a therapist, I understand that depression can present itself in various forms. Some people can't get out of bed and function in their normal day to day routine while others get up every single day and function just fine externally but maybe not so much internally. Have you ever experienced depression symptoms? If so, how did you handle that season of your life?

2. Sometimes changing your perspective is easier said than done. What are some challenges to changing our own perspective?

3. Try this the next time you notice yourself getting frustrated with a situation. Imagine yourself being able to fly. First, fly up to the ceiling and observe your situation, then fly outside of the building and observe your situation, then fly 30 thousand feet in the air like a plane and observe your situation, then fly into outer space where you can look down and see planet Earth and observe your

situation. By this time you should realize that your problem isn't as big as it looked at first. Take deep breaths during this entire imagery exercise.

CHAPTER 5
NO ROOM FOR FEAR

I went skiing for the first time March 2013 in Montreal, Canada. My mother and I were rookies at skiing, so we chose to get on the beginner slope. It was still steep for beginners if you ask me! We get all suited up, and the excitement is just running through my veins. Before we get on the lift, I ask the man an elementary, but essential, things such as how to stop and turn. Later we found out that we were supposed to take classes before skiing. I'm pretty sure that is where they teach you how to stop.

Nevertheless, we are there and ready to ski so we take the lift to the top of the mountain and we wobble out of the seat and inch our way towards the edge right before we hit the point of no return. The excitement quickly shifts to fear! I stare down the hill for about 5 minutes trying to figure out how to get down all in one piece. I see other people just scoot on down, falling and all, but fear has a tight grip on my legs. I realized I couldn't stand there forever, and the only way down was down the hill, so I take the first step, and I'm finally in motion. I started off skiing towards the snow wall because it gave me a sense of comfort that I could have something to run into in the event of an emergency.

Sure enough, I did. I didn't know how to turn so into the wall I went. Bam! I hit the ground very hard and burst into deep laughter. I think I was overjoyed more at the fact that falling didn't hurt like I thought it would. Where is my mom at this point? Oh, she had already fallen and took off her skis to walk the rest of the way down. She was so over it, but she only did it because of me! Mom power!

Fear Lied to Me

I survived the first trip down, and I decided to venture back up the lift to give it a second try. I felt a little bit more confident, so I jumped right in and about halfway down…Bam! I plopped again but this time harder. It was hard enough for my skis to go flying off! I was okay though, thank you for your concern. From that moment on though, I did not fall anymore. I was able to maneuver more towards the middle of the hill, and I was able to swivel left and right to add some fun to it. I realized that the less time I gave myself to be fearful the better I got, and the quicker I got to the bottom of the hill without falling. So instead of standing at the mountaintop feeling afraid, I jumped off that lift, quickly scooted to the edge and just went for it.

Away with Fear

Fear is meant to handicap you and cause you to feel that what is ahead of you is too large for you to handle. Your fear is then confirmed as you wobble down the path, that you questioned in the first place, and smash against the wall. Fear told you not to go, and your face against the wall and in the ground confirmed that notion. BUT, the moment you ignore fear and stand up a little bit straighter you realize that it isn't that hard or scary after all! Feeding your fear only gives you a self-fulfilling prophecy that says you can't do it and never should have attempted. Once I conquered my fear, I stood at the top with a winning mindset knowing that I could master that challenge without failing again!

Stop letting fear dictate what you can and cannot do! The more you feed your fear, the more you will receive "confirmation" that you cannot do it and should never attempt again! Instead, you need to (1) stand strong, (2) remember the instructions you were given, (3) have a winning mindset, (4) remember that if God told you to do it then you CAN and He has already equipped you with everything you need to do it with Him by your side, (5) stop looking for alternative ways to do what you were told to do (no walking down if you were meant to ski down), and (6) just go and do it! Simple as that!

Simple Nuggets

- Fear only makes the assignment that God gives you seem impossible.
- Fear slows you down.
- The longer you dwell on reasons "why" you can't do something the more you are allowing fear to set in and build up.
- Ten times out of ten what you fear concerning the assignment of your life is non-existent.
- The easiest way to overcome fear is to do the very thing causing you fear.
- What you are afraid to do is probably a good indicator that that is the very thing you should be doing.

Mission Possible

What did it take for this mission to be accomplished? Take some time to read the prayers and scriptures below.

Here are a couple of things it took:

- Persistence- Lord, give me the strength to not grow weary in doing what you have called me to do. Help me to persevere and never to give up.
  - *"Blessed is the one who perseveres under trial because, having stood the test, that person will receive the crown of life that the Lord has promised to those who love him." – James 1:12 (NIV)*
- Boldness & Courage- Lord, give me the boldness and courage that You had when You stood against Your enemies. Give me the courage to stand even if my circumstances are giving me every reason to tuck my tail and run.
  - *"Have I not commanded you? Be strong and of good courage;do not be afraid, nor be dismayed,*

for the Lord your God is with you wherever you go." – Joshua 1:9

- Refusal to fear- Lord, remind me that fear does not come from You so if I do fear, it is a lie. Help me to be bold in stepping out into the unknown.
  - *"For God has not given us a spirit of fear, but of power and of love and of a sound mind." - II Timothy 1:7*
  - *"The Lord is my light and my salvation; whom shall I fear? The Lord is the strength of my life; of whom shall I be afraid?" – Psalm 27:1*

Reflection Questions

1. When it comes to your destiny and doing the impossible, what causes you fear?
2. What does this fear prohibit you from doing?
3. Are you more committed to your fear or your future? Whichever one you allow to win and whichever one you focus on the most is your answer.

CHAPTER 6
SPEAK UP AND ASK

I recall waking up one morning feeling joyful, but then something happened that I did not like, so my joy dropped a bit. I started grumbling and complaining saying things like, "Ugh, I was fine before all of this happened" and stuff like that. You know, the usual complainer statements. So as I was sulking around the house pouting, God wanted me to talk to Him about it, but I told Him, "It's okay, I don't wish to talk about this right now." While attempting to avoid talking about it, the Holy Spirit reminded me of a message from a bible study message. The pastor was talking about the story of Peter walking on water[1]. I had never paid attention to this, but the pastor was showing us how Jesus was watching Him as he was going down UNTIL he opened up his mouth to ask for help and at that moment Jesus responded IMMEDIATELY.

> *"But when he saw that the wind was boisterous, he was afraid; and beginning to sink he cried out, saying, "Lord, save me!" [31] And immediately Jesus stretched out His hand and caught him, and said to him, "O you of little faith, why did you doubt?"* – Matthew 14:30-31

Stop Drowning Unnecessarily

I didn't want to sink any lower unnecessarily, so with this word in mind I decided to talk to God about how I was feeling. After venting, He then asked me, "What do you want?" and I told Him. People I kid you not, shortly after finally telling Him what I wanted I got confirmation from a friend that what I desired, He would do. I just needed to trust Him.

I am not so sure why we as believers can sometimes be so timid in asking God for things as if

He is some big bad wolf that will huff and puff at every request and desire that we make. I think for me, I use to avoid asking because I didn't want to ask for something that I shouldn't be asking for (what we think is good for us is not always good for us). So my fear of asking was solely due to the fear of asking for the wrong things.

So when I asked Him I said, "If this is in your will then I want XYZ..." and He responded positively to my request. I think we also don't ask because we have a little thought in the back of our mind that says, " I know He CAN do it but WILL He do it?" It just helps to realize that if He doesn't do it or give it to us, then it probably wasn't in His will, or the timing just isn't right.

Be Careful What You Ask For

I do believe there is permissive will and free will so we can get things and it not necessarily be His will but we get it because of our choices. Have you ever wanted to be with somebody so much but once you finally got him or her you thought, "return to sender!" Or, have you ever begged to get a job but once you got it you hated waking up every morning to go? It is my firm belief that those people with a strong relationship with God, can literally ask for things and He automatically does them just because of the relationship they have. I'll take it a step further and say, that same person can simply think of something they desire, and God does it because it is their internal desire. When this happens it reminds me of Isaiah 65:24, *"It shall come to pass that before they call, I will answer; and while they are still speaking, I will hear."*

Does that make the saying, "a closed mouth doesn't get fed" still true? I'm sure it still has its place, but I'd like to add that a closed mind doesn't get fed either. A closed mouth may not get fed, but a spiritually open and receptive mind will. There have been times where I would just think a thing, and God would honor it, but then there have been times when God has literally told me, like you tell a child, "open your mouth and use your words to tell me what you want." *"Death and life are in the power of the tongue, and those who love it will eat its fruit[2]."* You will eat the fruit of your words, so I sure hope you are making them tasty!

Guard Your Mouth

Your mission will require that you guard your words like they are life; because they are. If the impossible isn't turning into the possible for you, then check your mouth. What have you been speaking internally and externally? Are you saying you can one minute and you can't the next? Those are inconsistent declarations so don't be surprised if you don't see any fruit. It is like planting a seed and then digging it up the next day, and then replanting it the next, only to change your mind and go back and dig it up again. It'll never take root so don't expect any fruit.

He's Listening

God moves when we speak so don't be afraid to go to Him and tell Him ALL about the desires of your heart. He is listening, and He does care. As a reminder from the introduction, the closer you get to God the more blended you will notice His desires and your desires will become. So in essence, when you are asking for things, it is the desire He has placed in you in the first place sooo, you are essentially asking for something He has already approved. Now that's a sweet deal, so ask with confidence and boldness!

Mission Possible

What did it take for this mission to be accomplished? Take some time to read the prayer and scriptures below.
Here is one thing it took:
- <u>An open mouth</u>- Lord, thank You for desiring to commune with me. I have so much to say, but I

am not quite sure how to say it or how to ask it. Please help me to know that I can be comfortable with You and that I can trust You with the desires of my heart. You care about all things concerning me, even my thoughts, so I give my desires and concerns over to You. I will trust you regardless if Your answer is something I want to hear or something I do not want to hear. I know that You have my best interest in mind!

- *"And whatever you ask in My name, that I will do, that the Father may be glorified in the Son."*
  – John 14:13
- *"And in that day you will ask Me nothing. Most assuredly, I say to you, whatever you ask the Father in My name He will give you."*
  – John 16:23
- What else did it take?

Reflection Questions

1. What do you have in your heart that you are too timid to ask God?
2. What would be the worst that could happen if you ask? Him saying no isn't all THAT bad…at least you asked!
3. If life and death are in the power of the tongue, then that speaks volumes about the importance of our mouth. It is a powerful weapon. Have you ever spoken or thought something and it happened? Write about that experience.

CHAPTER 7
DON'T TAKE NO FOR AN ANSWER

What do you mean, no?

I have learned that there are three categories of no's when it comes to the fulfillment of your destiny. There is (1) No- this means, no. Point blank. It means move on to something else. It doesn't mean maybe. It means no. Then you have (2) No, not yet. It means a yes will soon follow but the time is not right now. It means to be still and wait. In ready, set, go it would be the set. Use this time for preparation for what is to come soon. Finally, you have (3) No, not that. Sometimes God says no because what we asked for was too small. Or, sometimes we miss the mark, and God says, "close but not quite." It is important to know what your "no's" mean so that you know whether you need to move on or whether you need to persist.

Persistence Pays Off

Your mission possible journey will require grit and persistence from you. You may encounter some resistance and push back but that does not mean what you are doing won't work or is not right. I recall wanting to work for a company a few years ago. I submitted my application online but didn't hear anything back after a month. So I found the person's contact information that worked in Human Resources. I ended up speaking to her assistant but not to her. Still, nothing came of it, so I waited a couple more weeks and tried emailing again. Still, no response so I waited about a month or so and decided to give it one more try. I gave her another call, and she answered. She asked if I could come in for an interview the next day and I did. After a great two-hour interview I walked out with the position. This situation really just boiled down to, "how bad do you want it?!" If you want it bad enough, you will be persistent.

I also had another similar situation where I knew I didn't fully qualify for the job so I knew I had to be very quick and persistent and give them all of the reasons to say yes before they could tell me no! I filled out the online application. As soon as I did that, I emailed my resume and cover letter to the director of the department. After I did that, I picked up the phone to tell her that I just applied online and also had just sent her an email. She truly appreciated me giving her that added touch.

She told me that she wasn't the one scheduling the interviews though, so I found out who was. And you guessed it; I emailed the lady doing the hiring and then called to leave a voice message to tell her that I did. I knew they were already interviewing people that week so I had to move quickly.

She hadn't called me back the next day, so I printed my resume and cover letter, which she already had 20 copies by now, but that's not the point.

I stop by the office the next day and ask to speak with her. She wasn't there, but her assistant was so she came out to meet me. It was great because she told me what they were looking for but it hadn't been indicated on my resume or application. So I gathered all the information she told me they would want to know and I immediately emailed it to her and everyone I had been in contact with at this point. And guess what, I finally get a response to my email that next day. She asks if I can do a phone interview the next day and I can. We have the interview, and she then asks if I can come in for a second interview with the rest of the team. I have the interview, and they offer me the job.

I knew that the odds would be stacked against me, especially if they were going strictly by what they required. I didn't have everything they required, but I sure was going to make saying no to me very hard. One way or the other they were going to know that I work hard for what I want, I am persistent, I know how to persevere, and I don't take limits or unmet requirements as an excuse to not try. I am persistent when I know something is my YES. If God had told me to stop and move on, I would've done it in a heartbeat, but because I knew He said I could have it, I didn't take no (or silence) for an answer.

When Your Yes Turns to a No

I was completely confused the first time I had a yes turn to a no. Before I got into a relationship with this guy I prayed and asked God if I could or not. God tells me yes so we begin dating. The first half of the relationship was great, but it started to take a downhill turn. It was a relationship that truly challenged me to make some personal changes that were necessary.

Towards the last few months, things were often tense, and I began to sense that it was time for it to come to an end. I decided to end it, but I was still heartbroken about it. I cried to God asking Him how something He told me to get into could fail. His response was straightforward, " It was my will for you to get in the relationship and it was also my will for you to get out of it."

This didn't make sense to me at first though. I figured if He said yes then that means yes forever. Therefore, I was stumped when my yes turned to a no. But I knew that He was intentional, so I tried to find the win in what felt like a failure.

One thing that He was teaching me was how to continually listen to His voice because He could choose to give new instructions at any time. Abraham and Isaac are a great example of this. God first told Abraham to kill Isaac, but just as Abraham was getting ready slay his son, God spoke and said no[1]! Abraham's yes changed to a no really quickly so had he only listened to the first set of instructions, he would have killed what God intended to live.

Mission Possible

What did it take for this mission to be accomplished? Take some time to read the prayer and scripture below.

Here is one thing it took:

- <u>Discernment</u>- Lord, put me in the Gym of Discernment so that my senses are strengthened. Help me to be able to hear your voice and heed your instructions accurately.
  - *"But solid food belongs to those who are of full age, that is, those who by reason of use have their senses exercised to discern both good and evil." – Hebrews 5:14*
- What else did it take?

Reflection Questions

1. Have you ever had a no turn into a yes or a yes turn into a no? What happened? How did you handle it?
2. Have you ever done something that you were told NOT to? What happened?
3. How do you handle no's and not yet's? What goes on mentally and emotionally for you when you are told to wait?

CHAPTER 8
WALK ON FAITH

When I think about faith, I recall a story from my freshman year in college. Some friends introduced me to a conference called IMPACT conference, and while it sounded fascinating, I just wasn't sure if I wanted to go. As time was winding down, I finally decided to go at the last minute. Had I registered earlier, I would have gotten a better discount but because I registered so late I had to pay the regular price. I really wanted to pay the discounted rate though, so I decided to contact the person over registration to see if I could get the same freshman rate even though I was late. I sent her an email and told her my story and the reasons for deciding so late. I mentioned in the email that I was standing on faith that I would still be able to get the freshman rate.

She didn't respond right away, and I didn't want to be later than I already was so I went ahead and registered and paid the deposit fee to hold my spot. I went ahead and paid because although she hadn't emailed and said yes, I still believed that when she did finally reply she would say yes.

Sure enough, a few days later I get a call from her, and she said yes! It wasn't just a simple "Ok sure" conversation either. She took the time to tell me that the only reason she said yes was that she saw that I went ahead and paid my deposit and that showed her that I truly was going to stand on faith and take the first step.

I am convinced that if I had not already paid the deposit, she would have said no. Why? Because I would have had nothing to show that my faith was real. An action followed by my words sealed the deal, so to speak. I took action on my faith, and it was honored and looked upon as pleasing.

Perfect Your Faith

I love the passage, James 2:14-26, that discusses how faith without works is dead. This passage supports my story very well. Verse 22, in particular, primarily confirms that both work together to get the job done. It reads, *" [22] Do you see that faith was working together with his works, and by works faith was made perfect?"* Don't tell me you have faith if you are not DOING anything to prove your faith! In Hebrews 11 all of those people mentioned, that were deemed righteous for their faith, DID SOMETHING to support their belief.

Don't tell me your faith...show me your faith! Have you or someone you've been talking to ever said, "do you see what I am saying?" while trying to explain something? We should SEE what you are SAYING. And that is how you perfect your faith.

> *"Therefore, since we are surrounded by such a great cloud of witnesses, let us throw off everything that hinders*

and the sin that so easily entangles. And let us run with perseverance the race marked out for us, ^{2} fixing our eyes on Jesus, the pioneer and perfecter of faith. For the joy set before him he endured the cross, scorning its shame, and sat down at the right hand of the throne of God. ^{3} Consider him who endured such opposition from sinners, so that you will not grow weary and lose heart."
- Hebrews 12:1-3.

This verse reminds us to run our race and work our faith.

What About Grace and Favor

Of course, there are two sides to a coin. God has blessed me with stuff that I didn't even ask for so I know it wasn't my faith and works that got it for me. It was simply God's grace and favor and His desire to bless me. There have even been seasons in my life where the Lord wanted me just to be still and simply trust Him to do what He said. My job, my "works" if you will, were to simply quiet my spirit and believe that He can do what He promised. Then after that season was up, I could feel Him transitioning me to a season where I would take more action. I think the first one was the hardest to do because I am a natural "doer" so to be told to stop doing and learn how to "be" was very hard. If you are a "fix it yourself" kind of guy or gal then maybe the works that you need to combine with your faith is letting go and letting God handle it. You just have to discern which He is asking you to do at this time.

When Faith Hurts

I understand what it's like to take a hard blow on your faith. It knocks you off balance and makes you momentarily question why you even believe for that thing in the first place. But I had to come to a mental place of, "what's the worst that could happen if I continue to have faith?" The worst that I could think of was, "well what if it DOESN'T happen!? What if I DO get my HOPES up?" *Hope deferred makes the heart sick, but when the desire comes, it is a tree of life[1].*

Have you ever just been so sick of faith? Have you ever just got to the point where you are tired of having expectations and then those expectations disappointed? I'll raise my hand and say yes. But I had to get over my feelings and understand that if I didn't hope for anything, then I couldn't have faith for anything[2], and if I didn't have faith, then I couldn't please my Father. I was willing to take the pain of a disappointment over disappointing Daddy God. And honestly, the closer I stay to Him now, the less daunting any disappointments are because I KNOW that He is a good Daddy and I KNOW He will not withhold any good thing from me[3]. So if He says no or if He takes it away from me, instead of complaining, I whisper, "I trust that You know what You are doing."

Mission Possible

What did it take for this mission to be accomplished? Take some time to read the prayers and scriptures below.

Here are a couple of things it took:

- <u>Faith</u>- Lord, I believe You to do the things You said You'd do, but please help my unbelief. Help me to trust that You are not a man so you cannot lie. Help me to stand firm on Your word even when I can't see what You've promised.
  - *"But without faith it is impossible to please Him, for he who comes to God must believe that He is, and that He is a rewarder of those who diligently seek Him." – Hebrews 11:6*
- <u>Action</u>- Lord, help me to discern my current season. Help me to know whether You want me to "do" or to "be." Give me the strength to put in the work to show You that I am serious about what You've promised me.
  - *"But someone will say, "You have faith, and I have works." Show me your faith without your works,*

and I will show you my faith by my works. ^{19} You believe that there is one God. You do well. Even the demons believe—and tremble! ^{20} But do you want to know, O foolish man, that faith without works is dead?" – James 2:14-8-20

- What else did it take?

Reflection Questions

1. Have you ever had faith in something that didn't happen the way you had in mind? What was your response to the situation?
2. What are you currently believing to happen? What works have you combined to match that faith?
3. Are you a doer? If so, what makes "just being" and not fixing it yourself challenging for you?

CHAPTER 9
IT TAKES VULNERABILITY

I was reading one of my journal entries back from January 2013, and during that time God had been speaking to me about being open about who I was, my struggles, my flaws, and all. I was processing His request by reflecting on how I would prefer to follow someone who is transparent and willing to show others how they made it through. God confirmed this thought after a friend, and I went ice-skating. I skated around a few times just having a good ole time. I did end up falling; only once though. Once we got tired, we decided to take a break and just watch others skate.

There was this extremely skilled skater out there and we just ooh'd and aah'd each time he passed by doing some ridiculously difficult jump or spin. But then the moment happened. He does another spin and lands smack dab on his butt! When he fell, I leaned into my friend and said, "It makes me feel better when I see the really great skaters fall." Now, I didn't say this in such a way to laugh at his moment of failure, but I said it as a way of encouraging myself. There were many less skilled people out there falling, and there were plenty of children falling all over the place, but the "expert" skater falling had the most impact on me. Why? Because it showed me that even the best of us could fall sometimes, and it's okay as long as we get back up and keep trucking along.

Vulnerability is Necessary

If I had to choose, I would prefer a person with a testimony and some struggles in her life to tell me that I can make it through compared to someone who has had a 100% perfect life (or so they say). It is so funny how God gives you an opportunity to act on the revelation He has given you and gives you a chance to practice your own preaching. Back in 2013, I was in the process of being a guest writer for this particular website, and I asked what they would like for me to write. The editor responded and asked if I could write something nitty-gritty from my own life and share something that God brought me through that made Him seem more real.

For some reason I got those nervous flutters in my belly. I have much to talk about that God has brought me through but the moment of truth isn't so appealing after all when it is your own stuff that you are exposing. Being open, honest, and truthful about our own lives and struggles can be a very uncomfortable and difficult thing for each of us to do. However, what good is it if God continues to do great things in your life and delivers you time after time yet you fail to share the goodness with others? We are supposed to share the good news, right? Your testimony is good news of the greatness of God, your forgiveness is good news of God's sovereignty, your salvation is good news of God's love, your healing and deliverance is good news of

God's miraculous hand, your freedom is good news of God's redemptive power, and your blessings and protection are good news of God's grace & mercy. Though uncomfortable, be the light in somebody's dark situation and share of how God became real to you.

But Vulnerability is Scary

Vulnerability hasn't always been my strong suit. In the past, I preferred to be strong, save face, and say "I'm okay" even if everything wasn't okay. Truthfully, I just didn't want to allow people that close to me to know all of my business. I use to say I'm private but that no longer works when you are still "private" with the those closest to you.

I remember the director of my program asking me how my experience was in the classroom. I just broke down crying out of nowhere. In my head I'm thinking, "girl, pull yourself together" but the tears kept flowing. I dried my eyes and explained how those few years had been tough because I did desire to have close relationships with my classmates but one student ruined that opportunity. Well, it turned out for my good in the end.

A quick rabbit trail about that. In our first semester, we had a small group discussion with everyone in our cohort. I was usually very quiet or kept everything surface when I did talk about myself. One girl got irritated with that, so she calls me out in front of the group and says that she thinks I am fake. Yep, that's what she said. I'm sure there was a better way of saying it but what she was trying to express was how she felt I was not vulnerable and how unwilling I was to let my guard down. I was infuriated at her for saying it, but three years later we were able to have a restorative conversation about it. Although it hurt, she had a point. I wasn't vulnerable, and that isn't very attractive to people who sincerely want to see your heart. Her comment helped to spark my vulnerability journey.

Ok, back off the rabbit trail and fast forward those three years back into my director's office. I continue talking about my experience, and I tell her that for those three years after her comment, I felt isolated. I'd admit that I was very standoffish from just about everyone; because of her. The director listens intently, and then thanks me for my tears. Now of course my tears have already embarrassed me so my face changes from sad to confused. Why was she thanking me for crying?! She goes on to explain by saying that my tears were a gift to her. They allowed her to see me. They gave her a moment inside of my 10 feet tall wall. They allowed her to look beyond my resume and accolades. She even said that she now felt even closer to me and liked me all the more because of it.

I left out of that meeting feeling much lighter and with a new revelation. Vulnerability isn't a weakness; it's the doorway to having genuine and authentic relationships. I learned that people draw closer to transparent and real people; not superhero people. Superheroes feel untouchable, and all people want to know is, "are you relatable?" I didn't want to show my vulnerability because I wanted her to think

I was strong. But fake strength was a huge turn off! I became more likable when I was real.

Mission Possible

What did it take for this mission to be accomplished? Take some time to read the prayers and scriptures below.

Here are a couple of things it took:

- <u>Honesty</u>- Lord, at times it is difficult to be open and honest with other people and there are times when it may even be difficult to be honest with you. Help me to practice being vulnerable by starting with you. Help me to reveal the hidden places in my heart to You.
  - *"And He said to me, "My grace is sufficient for you, for My strength is made perfect in weakness." Therefore most gladly I will rather boast in my infirmities, that the power of Christ may rest upon me." – II Corinthians 12:9*
- <u>A safe place to be vulnerable</u>- Lord, help me to put aside my pride and "togetherness- face" to

help others who need it. Give me the boldness to be vulnerable about my life and how You have brought me through. Thank You for using the negative moments in my life as a blessing in another person's life. I am grateful knowing that I can help others simply by sharing my testimony.

- *"Fear not, for I am with you; be not dismayed, for I am your God. I will strengthen you, yes, I will help you, I will uphold you with My righteous right hand."*

  – Isaiah 41:10

- What else did it take?

Reflection Questions

1. What are some things that God has brought you through that you know will benefit so many others?
2. Remember that we do not only go through for the development of ourselves but also for others as well!
    a. So, who's breakthrough, deliverance, or blessing is tied to you sharing God's power in your own life?
3. Is being vulnerable tough for you? If yes, write about what makes it difficult in your journal.

CHAPTER 10
YOU ARE NOT IN IT ALONE

I recall not feeling my usual "upbeat self" one Sunday morning after church in Nashville. So I go home, eat lunch, and take about a 3-hour nap. I woke up, but I still didn't feel upbeat, and I couldn't quite put my finger on it, but my spirit was off balance. I wanted to get to the bottom of it, so I got up and decided to go to my prayer closet and pray.

I started asking questions about certain things and found myself getting irritated. So much so that I couldn't even focus on praying, so my eyes begin to wander around, and I see a book that I had lying on the floor called "Captivating: Unveiling the Mystery of a Woman's Soul" by John & Stasi Eldredge.

I picked it up and felt a nudge to turn to a certain page. I started reading with an "ugh I already know this" kind of attitude, but I suddenly find myself in tears.

Drop Your Weapons

This particular segment that I was instructed to turn to first started by talking about a passage from Hosea 2:6-7 and how Jesus has to get anything out of the way that is blocking us from completely seeking after Him for all of our needs. Then John & Stasi go on and provide an example of one lady who shared her testimony, and it said, *"...because of the defensiveness I buried my truly feminine heart which longs so deeply to be pursued and fought for, to be seen as beautiful...I stand now in this risky place of vulnerability, with a bleeding heart waiting and praying." (p 97-98)*[1]

I began to cry because I was able to see myself in this woman's testimony. In my past, I used to portray myself as this woman that had everything together and a woman that let nothing get to her. I was so accustomed to being "Miss Independent" and "Sista Soldier" especially when it came to a relationship or friendship with a man.

I used to say "don't worry about it...I can do it myself" because that is just the type of woman that I had grown to be. I hadn't had a chance to truly put my guard down and be a vulnerable, feminine, and willing to be pursued type of woman who needed a defender.

Why Do You Have to Be So Strong?

I use to view being a strong woman as a beautiful thing. And it is, don't get me wrong, but if that strength is trying to overpower the strength that God wants to show us, then it isn't so beautiful after all. God wants to be our rescuer, our defender, and our protector and if our guards are constantly up and if we are continually finding safety in other things then we are holding on to the wrong strength.

After reading this portion of the book, I was then able to understand why I wasn't so upbeat after leaving the church. The sermon had been tugging at some unresolved problems that my spirit was picking up. The message was titled "It Won't End That Way," and it came from Ezekiel 16:6-9. The pastor was talking about how Jesus passes by us in our own life and sees us lying in our own "blood," but He stops by and tells us to live and then He covers us. Bishop Walker III mentioned three reasons why we bleed: (1) our own personal failures (i.e., poor decisions), (2) other people's foolishness (i.e., bad relationships), and (3) God's providence (i.e., wanting to mature us).

Tear Those Walls Down

It all came full circle for me after picking up that book *Captivating*. I realized that I was also a woman who was still walking around living life but with a bleeding heart. I was bleeding from all the unvisited and buried wounds that others had caused. The ones that I just brushed under the rug and said, "I won't worry about it, it doesn't bother me, I will forget them in no time." When in reality I didn't. The toughness that I had was due to all of the expectations that each male, time after time had yet to meet. There were those that said they would be there but were nowhere to be found, those that said they would protect me, but left me open to hurt, and those that said they would come back for me...but still I waited.

It took me some time, but I finally realized why I was a "do it myself" type of woman. I felt that since very few of the men I had ever dated in the past truly protected me, I had to do it myself. And that is when the walls came up. [*Side note: I also did realize that I was the common denominator in these relationships, so I had to take an honest self-assessment to figure out what was going on inside of me and what my role was in each failed relationship. I talk about this more in my second book titled The Caged in Heart: How Your Childhood Wounds are Affecting Your Adult Life*].

God had opened an invitation to me in that prayer closet for me to allow Him to be my rescuer, the one who pursues me, the one who will save me, the one who will love me unconditionally, the one who will be everything that I had never had and more! It was on that night that I accepted His intimate invitation to trust Him more. I didn't realize how me being so used to guarding, covering, and defending myself without a man was showing up in my relationship with God.

God is extending this same invitation to you, man and woman. The walls you've put up are blocking your primary connection to the possible. Without this main link, nothing is possible. Your wall will soon crumble on its own anyway, and sometimes it is a hard fall but wouldn't it be better for you to take it down brick by brick voluntarily? The impossible is made possible when you and the Lord are in sync with one another. Having a wall up prevents synchronicity. It is like trying to tango with someone who has a huge moving box strapped to his or her chest. It makes connecting challenging, thus not creating the bond it takes to dance correctly. Drop your defenses and let Him in closer. It is in this wall-free state that the possible can freely occur.

Mission Possible

What did it take for this mission to be accomplished? Take some time to read the prayers and scriptures below.

Here are a couple of things it took:

- <u>Surrendering your heart to Him</u>- Lord, I surrender my heart to you. I ask that you tear down the walls I have built around my heart. Bring you and me closer together. So much so that we become one. I in You and You in me.
  - *"Trust in the LORD with all your heart, and lean not on your own understanding; ^{6} in all your ways acknowledge Him, and He shall direct your paths." – Proverbs 3:5-6*
- <u>Surrendering your strength for His</u>- Lord, thank you for being the awesome Dad and male figure that I need in my life. Thank you for your

relentless and unconditional love! I thank you for pursuing me and never stopping! Now I surrender my all to you. I put down my defenses and am willing to allow myself to be vulnerable with you…the way that you created me to be.

- *"I will love You, O Lord, my strength. ² The Lord is my rock and my fortress and my deliverer; my God, my strength, in whom I will trust; my shield and the horn of my salvation, my stronghold." – Psalm 18:1-2*

- What else did it take?

Reflection Questions

1. Do you have any unresolved problems in your life that you have left under the rug that needs to be re-visited for healing? Have an honest conversation with God about your hurts/pains/wounds and invite Him in to heal you and to break those lies that you have held on to for so long.
2. Have you truly made God your primary source in every aspect of your life?
3. How does your relationship with others show in your relationship with God? For example, I was walled in with men and so was I with God.

CHAPTER 11
INCONVENIENCES ARE YOUR BEST FRIEND

This is Not What I Signed Up For

November 19, 2017, was my very first Dallas Cowboys game. My mom and nephew had flown in town so we went and got all of our paraphernalia and we were ready and excited to go. We arrived super early, or so we thought, but the traffic was super crazy already. So we venture to move as close to the stadium as we could. Being our first game, we didn't know that you couldn't just pay cash for a parking decal. We see a guy yelling about having parking passes so we roll the window down and he tells us how much and where we could park. We were not trying to park far so we kept confirming that he gave a close park. Of course, he is just nodding, pointing, and saying, "yes, it's right across the street over there."

As we approach the lot that he said was ours, I look down at the lot number on our ticket, and then I look at the actual lot number. They don't match. Gullible first-time gamers? Probably so. So at this point, we are looking out of the window in the area that we first saw him trying to find him to tell him to give us our $50 back because he lied to us. Our search could only go so far in traffic though so we gave up looking for him. I decided just to read the parking decal to see where our lot was. You guessed it. We were at one of the farthest lots out there.

You can only imagine the anger and frustration we all had. I mean we were complaining the entire way to the lot. We were complaining about the man, whining about how cold it is, and grumbling about how far we had to now walk in the cold. We were not happy campers. We finally get to our lot and find a park right near the entrance. At least we got close parking within the lot. I just so happened to look up and see a golf cart pull up. I assume it is for the lot people like us, so I run to the cart and hold it until my mom and nephew come. Phew. That settles at least one of our complaints. We no longer had to walk a million miles to get back to the stadium.

The golf cart driver pulls up to the stadium and drops us off at the golf cart designated space. As soon as we get off, an employee of the stadium asks us if we had just got off the golf cart. We said yes, and she points us in the direction of which line was ours. I kid you not. The line that she directs us to had NO line. We just walk up, give her our tickets, and we are free to walk in. It took all of 2 minutes if that. We walked past ALL of the people who had probably been standing in line for a minimum of 30 minutes. You would have thought we were three kids at Disney World. Each of us was smiling from ear to ear just laughing and hugging each other as we walked inside.

That ONE parking pass that we DID NOT want set us up for blessings that completely erased all of our complaints and brought joy to our hearts INSTANTLY. We realized just how much God blessed us, so we started laughing at just how silly we were even to complain. We started making jokes about how ridiculous we sounded when we were whining.

In retrospect, God was working out every last detail of that entire experience but we were so frustrated with the process because it wasn't what we had signed up for! We thought we had signed up for a close park not one across the city! But guess who automatically became forever grateful for that parking spot? We all did! We shifted from being infuriated about it to being overly joyed about it. It wasn't what we signed up for, but it sure was way better!

This is the Wrong Thing

As you can already begin to see, inconveniences aren't that bad after all. Here is another story to illustrate that. It was Thanksgiving Eve 2017, and my mom and I were at home cooking for the next day. My mom realized that we had forgotten to buy the piecrust for our sweet potato pies. So my dad is already out of the house, so she calls to tell him to stop by the store to bring some pie shells home. She emphasizes that she wants the frozen kind.

He finally gets home with the shells, and she takes them out of the bag, but he had bought the wrong ones. You could tell she was a little frustrated because she wanted the frozen ones, not the gram cracker crust ones. But we used them anyways because we had no other choice; the stores were all closed. We bake the pies, and once they cool off, we cut a slice to see how it turned out. OMG! That was the best sweet potato pie! It tasted way better than the frozen crust sweet potato pie that we normally make.

Now, of course, this is a week after our Dallas Cowboys experience, so we look at each other and laugh because we realize God is up to something. This was now the second time where He showed us that an inconvenience wasn't a negative thing. If you know anything about God, He does things in patterns so if something keeps reoccurring, pay attention. He has our full attention in that kitchen, so we say, "Ok God you are trying to teach us something. We are here and open to learning the lesson."

We know that God was, for one, showing us how we typically respond to things that we don't want; which was with irritation. But this second time around we realized that we don't have to get irritated when things don't go our way. All we have to do is trust that all things will work for our good. God was also showing us that He can and will bless us in ways that we didn't expect or in ways that we didn't even think were right! The matter of the fact is that the pie crust, plain and simple, was the wrong one. But the wrong one tasted better than the right one. God gave us a taste of just how much things with Him are sweeter if we just go with His flow! And for Christmas, we made the pies again, and this time we intentionally bought the gram cracker crust shells! Yum!

What I Wanted Rejected Me

I will share one more example of which I am proud to say that this go round I was ready to pass the "inconvenience" test. Whoohoo! Third times a charm I guess. So I was working with this woman on a project, and we had already had about two months under our belt working together as a team. One day she tells me that she thinks both of our personalities combined do not make a good fit. She goes on to explain why.

Come to find out; it wasn't our personalities that were the issue. She just had pint up anger that she never shared with me about this one thing I did that I was unaware had bothered her. I do have the gift of wisdom, discernment, and understanding but I do not read minds. [*Side note: when you are working with others, don't wait until you are so frustrated and irritated with a person before you finally tell them how they made you feel. Ongoing feedback is the better route to take. It could save the friendship/partnership.*] I didn't know how she felt until she told me she no longer wanted to work together. And it all boiled down to her not liking change.

I listened to her concerns, and I tried empathetically explaining to her that I did not know and that I wished she had told me when it first happened instead of when it was too late. I don't mind handling conflict, so I didn't leave flustered but I was slightly irritated when I did think about all of the time that now felt wasted and how I would have to search for a new team member. I got in my car right after the meeting, and I felt my head slightly drop, and I said in my mind, "ugh, this is an inconvenience!"

YES! There that word is again! The moment those words left my mouth I threw my head back with a big Kool-aid smile and said, "OMG, this is going to be so great! I can't wait to see what comes of it." The other previous experiences equipped me finally to see that good things can come from an inconvenience. And it did! I did what it took to locate a new opportunity, and I found one. And you guessed it, a better one than I had before.

Her rejection was merely God's redirection to take me on to bigger and better things. This applies especially well when talking about intimate relationships. It's okay if he or she rejects you. Let it go. Move on. Something bigger and better is on the way. So what if they said you were the problem, what's next will view you as a solution. Ironically enough, one of the women connected to this new opportunity asked me, "So how do you deal with change because things change a lot around here?" What was a problem for the first was non-negotiable for the second. It looks like I found the right place!

This Isn't What I Had in Mind

All of these experiences have taught me one simple thing. Just flow with God because He knows what He is doing. His thoughts and ways are well beyond our comprehension, and if we are trying to understand spiritual matters with our carnal mind, then we will miss it every single time. But if we step back and allow the Spirit to take control, we will find ourselves in the right place at the right time with the right people every single time!

So what if it is not what you had in mind! What you had in mind was probably too small anyways! If you plan to do the impossible, then you must be prepared for your small thoughts to be challenged and stretched often. No carnally minded person will jump up and say, "WhooHoo! This is so inconvenient this is great!" but a spiritually minded person who understands God's rerouting system undoubtedly will! If the Lord wants to inconvenience what I had in mind to give me something better I will be the first to sign up for that class, again!

Mission Possible

What did it take for this mission to be accomplished? Take some time to read the prayers and scriptures below.

Here are a couple of things it took:

- <u>Awareness of Him</u>- Lord, sometimes what I want can blind me from seeing the work that you are doing for me. Help me to call on You to get Heavenly insight when things don't seem to go my way.
  - *"Call to Me, and I will answer you, and show you great and mighty things, which you do not know." – Jeremiah 33:3*
- <u>Knowing that He always has a better plan</u>- Lord, help me to believe that You have a plan for my life. Help me to believe that You are attentive to every last detail of my day-to-day affairs. Help me to know that nothing just happens and that all things work for my good; even the things I don't like.
  - *"For I know the thoughts that I think toward you, says the LORD, thoughts of peace and not of evil, to give you a future and a hope."*
    -Jeremiah 29:11

- <u>Go with the flow</u>- Lord, help me to go with Your flow. Help me to submit my will to Yours. Help me to submit my desires to Your plan.
  - *"For as the heavens are higher than the earth, so are My ways higher than your ways, and My thoughts than your thoughts.* [10] *"For as the rain comes down, and the snow from heaven, and do not return there, but water the earth, and make it bring forth and bud, that it may give seed to the sower and bread to the eater,* [11] *So shall My word be that goes forth from My mouth; it shall not return to Me void, but it shall accomplish what I please, and it shall prosper in the thing for which I sent it." – Isaiah 55:9-11*
- What else did it take?

Reflection Questions

1. Has an inconvenience ever worked out for your good? Write about it.
2. Has a rejection ever worked out for your good? Write about it.
3. Has the "wrong thing" ever worked out for your good? Write about it.

CHAPTER 12
DEVELOP YOUR FORESIGHT

I have heard that hindsight is always 20/20. For those that do not know what this means here is a definition. "Hindsight is 20/20" is a phrase used after the fact; it is insight gained after something had happened that should have been obvious before it happened, but the person was not aware of it although the "clues" were there.

This whole concept began to bother me because it means that we had the information that we needed PRIOR to something happening, BUT we didn't adhere to it. Most people are able to use these moments as teachable moments but why bang your head against the wall to figure out if it will hurt you or not; especially if you do not have to?

I was telling a friend about this particular guy I was talking to in the past. I told her all about the dreams that I had about him; dreams that he was talking to other women at the same time as me (warning signs) and I told her about how I felt when I was around him (my spirit was always uneasy). Then I went on to tell her that we were no longer talking because come to find out he WAS talking to other women and he had his own selfish agenda with me. Her comment to all of this was, "well hindsight is always 20/20". This was so true, yet so painful to hear because all along I was given WARNING SIGNS about this guy but I IGNORED them ALL!

Ignoring What is Meant to Save You

Why did I ignore all of the warning signs though? Just like most of us do, I ignored them because they were not what I wanted to be true. I really liked this guy, and my emotions were in too deep, so I accused the devil of my negative dreams and uneasiness around him. Ha. Silly of me because there was nothing demonic about it and it had everything to do with God pointing certain things out to me and giving me warning signs ahead of time. He wanted to guard my heart and prevent me from wasting my time and going down the wrong road. He SHOWED me all of this, BUT I ignored it!

So I asked myself, "why do we wait for our 20/20 hindsight to kick in to learn and understand from an event? Why not work on our 20/20 foresight instead?" 20/20 foresight, to me, is HEEDING to all of the WARNING signs and LISTENING to them and doing something about them earlier on. On a scale of 0 to 10, we often know around 2 or 3 whether a person will be good for us or not. See Figure 1. Truthfully, our spirits can inform us that a person isn't right at a one, which would be automatically. So for example, a one would be those times when you first meet a person and with minimal, if any, conversation, you have already made up in your mind that you don't like that person, or you think, "I don't know what it is, but there is something about this person that I want to keep a look out for." This can happen both ways. You can meet a person for the first time and automatically like them and automatically sense their character. But for this section, we are talking about those negative warnings you receive. An example of a two or a three would be when they have now said or done something a few times to confirm what you were already feeling about them.

Figure 1

Your Gut Knows Best

I came across a video on social media of a young lady crying and talking about how she had just caught her fiancé cheating. She was heartbroken obviously because she loved him and they were planning a wedding. To add insult to injury, they just had a baby a few months back so not only is she broken about the relationship but she also now has to figure out how to be a single mom. I truly feel bad for her at this point. She then says, "but I should have known better because this is the fourth time he has cheated; each with different women."

Of course, I feel empathetic towards her, but the question did arise in my head of why didn't she just take the first cheat as a sign. I'm pretty sure he had other warning signs before the first cheat but why do we let things get to a 7, 8 or 9 before we finally pull the plug? Trust me, I have been there, done that, and have several plaques that read, "I stayed well past my time again." I rarely listened to that Holy Spirit gut nudge, but now I do because I know when He speaks, He is speaking for a reason. Some say I have a low tolerance, and I do, and some say I am quick to end a relationship before it even has a chance to get started, and I probably do, but I will repeat this, again and again, it has saved me time, energy, and unnecessary heart breaks.

I finally realized that Maya Angelou was right, *"When someone shows you who they are, believe them the first time."* I am a little more tolerant if it's just an annoying habit because those can change but if it is a fundamental issue with their character and heart, then I will gladly show them to the door, quickly. Habits are a little easier to change or just get over, but a person's heart is a person's heart. Yes, Jesus can renew their heart. Praise the Lord. So I will point them to Him and tell them to call me once He has made their heart new again. Amen. I've just learned that I'm nobody's savior, and I can't make anyone change but I know someone who can get you all the way together. His name is Jesus Christ! Not Trillion Small.

A "No" Could Save You

I have heard so many people say (including myself), "I just didn't know" or "I didn't expect that from them," or "I didn't see it coming" etc.… but I'm beginning to think that all of these are just lies! Sometimes we don't "see" the warning signs because we are not sensitive enough to God's voice and the many ways that He speaks to us, or we miss the warning signs simply because we choose to.

I was talking to a young lady about her recent breakup and she said that she knew she needed to end the relationship a long time ago, but she never wanted to pray and ask God if she should because she knew if He told her yes that she wouldn't want to. I guess that was a warning in and of itself. If you are afraid to talk to God about it, it may be something you shouldn't be doing anyways.

It's like being in high school and wanting to ask your mom if you could go to the homecoming party but you are so terrified of asking because you desperately want to go but are afraid of her response. So, instead of asking and hearing no, you just choose to sneak out of the house and end up arrested because there was underage drinking.

Her no would've crushed your little 17-year-old heart, but it would have also saved your little 17-year-old self from being arrested. Now matters have been made EVEN worse for you because now you have the fury of your mom. It would have been easier just to take the no and sit in your room and sulk for a few hours.

Silence Your Emotional Desires

Have your emotions ever gotten you into this kind of trouble? You just had to have that thing or person, and once you got it, it ended up causing you more headaches than the agony of desiring it was causing you. The heart can play tricks on you. It can cause us to see what isn't really there and it can cause us to ignore what is very apparent. Our desires can have us so coo coo for cocoa puffs that we drive down a proverbial freeway with all the flashing red lights and signs that say, "exit now, freeway ends!" but we are so blinded, so we keep driving until we fall off the cliff and then have the nerve to say, "I didn't know." Yes, you did. Open your eyes.

I share this with you, not to be hard on you but to save you time, energy, money, and unnecessary broken hearts. If you are getting warning signs about a mate (especially when considering marriage), then

LISTEN, if you are getting warning signs concerning making a sudden job or state move then LISTEN, if you are getting warning signs about hanging with a certain person or going to a certain place then LISTEN. Not only does listening save you time, energy, and emotions, it also can save your life!!!! So now when God tells you "no," simply say "thank you for having my best interest in mind" and move on. Get your eyes checked and tell Dr. Jesus, your Optometrist, that you want a prescription for 20/20 foresight and no longer will you depend solely on your 20/20 hindsight!

Here are a Few Things God Can Use to Warn You

- His word (which means you need to know what it says)
- The pastor (while sitting in service the message seems to be all in your business and hitting those particular areas)

- Holy Spirit (one way is by your gut feeling or lack of peace; which means you must be in an ongoing relationship with Him in order to recognize this feeling. Christmas, Mother's Day, and Easter just won't do)
- Other believers (your parents, friends, co-worker, boss, church member, etc. tell you)
- Dreams & Visions (while you are asleep or awake)
- Things in the natural (sometimes it is as simple as common sense such as the area not looking safe or they hide their phone often)

There could be other ways, so it is up to you to be sensitive at all times to God's gentle voice; in whichever form it may come. But remember this, wisdom, knowledge, and understanding is no good to you if you do not USE them.

Listening is crucial to your mission possible journey! If you do not heed to the voice of the Lord then how will you know what to do and what not to do? He knows the way that He takes you, so listen to His guidance and avoid unnecessary potholes!

Mission Possible

What did it take for this mission to be accomplished? Take some time to read the prayers and scriptures below.

Here are a couple of things it took:

- Protecting your heart- Thank You Lord for desiring to guard my heart in all that I do. I ask that You help me to be just as diligent in guarding my heart as You are.
  - *"Keep your heart with all diligence, for out of it spring the issues of life." - Proverbs 4:23*
- Listening- Thank You, Daddy, for clearing out my eyes and my ears so that I may hear You clearer in my life. Help me to obey what I hear You speak.
  - *"Do not merely listen to the word, and so deceive yourselves. Do what it says."*
    – James 1:22 (NIV)
- Intentional Maturity- Lord, as I spend more time with You, I know that how You speak to me will

become clearer. Help me to set aside more one-on-one time with You.

- o *"I have a lot more to say about this, but it is hard to get it across to you since you've picked up this bad habit of not listening. By this time you ought to be teachers yourselves, yet here I find you need someone to sit down with you and go over the basics on God again, starting from square one—baby's milk, when you should have been on solid food long ago! Milk is for beginners, inexperienced in God's ways; solid food is for the mature, who have some practice in telling right from wrong." – Hebrews 5: 11-14 (MSG)*

- <u>Trust in God's guidance</u>- Lord, remind me that You are a good Father who means well for me. Help me to trust Your "no" and know that it is for my good and not punishment.
- o *"Whether you turn to the right or to the left, your ears will hear a voice behind you, saying, "This is the way; walk in it." - Isaiah 30:21 (NIV)*
- What else did it take?

Reflection Questions

1. How has God been trying to get your attention in a particular situation?
2. Have you ever had this experience before where all of the "evidence"/"information" was right in front of you, but somehow you missed it? What happened?
3. What are the advantages of listening to the warning signs and what are the disadvantages of ignoring the warning signs?

EPILOGUE

The impossible is possible when you own it. To own something you must take possession of it. You must get a grip and a handle on it. Each of us is equipped to fulfill a different possible. Your gifts may not look like the next person's gifts if you both don't have the same destiny. When you discover Whose you are, you discover who you are. And when you discover who you are you discover what your own possible is.

Do not abort the mission. Your mission is your destiny, and your destiny is like your baby in the spirit. When you don't fulfill your mission, you don't give birth to what was inside of you.

Have faith, believe, remain close to the Lord, and walk the journey planned just for you and you will have what you have been called and anointed to produce. Remember, much root yields much fruit, little root yields little fruit, and no root yields no fruit. The condition of your heart and the state of your mind play a huge role in the depth of your root. A fertile heart and an open mind are ripe to birth the impossible.

A wise person once said, *"The sky is not the limit. Your belief system is."* You will not go where your mind does not permit you to go. As you grow and mature in the faith, many more things become more permissible. Your mind begins to realize that you do, in fact, have so much more to offer the world. As you renew your mind, your creativity will flow without restraint just like God. He is creative. And since you were made in His image, you are a creative being too.

We paint our world with our words. Color your world with things that are true, noble, just, pure, and lovely[1]. Color it with the things you want, not with the things you don't want. If you don't want it in your picture, don't paint it. The world is in need of the masterpiece you bring to the table so make haste and ready yourself. In order to change the world around you, you must change the world within you first. Get a hold of yourself and declare, "I AM POSSIBLE!"

Without faith, it is impossible to please God, and without God, nothing is possible.

CHAPTER NOTES

Introduction
   1. Matthew 6:10
   2. Matthew 19:26
   3. I Corinthians 12

Chapter 1
   1. Exodus 3:14
   2. Genesis 1:27
   3. Genesis 17
   4. Matthew 9:18-26
   5. Matthew 9:21

Chapter 2
   1. *Delivered at New Covenant Baptist Church, Chicago, Illinois, on 9 April 1967 (retrieved from http://kingencyclopedia.stanford.edu/encyclopedia/documentsentry/doc_the_three_dimensions_of_a_complete_life.1.html*
   2. Philippians 1:6

Chapter 3
   1. Revelation 19:10b

Chapter 6
   1. Matthew 14:22-33
   2. Proverbs 18:21

Chapter 7
   1. Genesis 22

Chapter 8
   1. Proverbs 13:12
   2. Hebrews 11:1

3. Psalm 84:11
   4. Chapter 10
   1. "Captivating: Unveiling the Mystery of a Woman's Soul" (2005). John & Stasi Eldredge. Pp. 97-98.

Epilogue
   1. Philippians 4:8

ABOUT THE AUTHOR

Dr. Trillion Small has a Ph.D. in Clinical Counseling and is a Licensed Marriage and Family Therapist. She is a TEDx Speaker. Her talk, which can be found on Youtube, is titled "Overcoming the Fear of Love". She is also the Founder/Lead Organizer for TEDxFrisco in Frisco, Texas. Additionally, Dr. Small is a certified John Maxwell coach. She is the author of several books and is the Founder/CEO of They Speak Publishing.

Dr. Small is passionate about youth development. She is the Executive Director for the 501(c)(3) Prepare Academy. Their focus is to personally and professionally prepare the next generation and equip the community to be emotionally & relationally intelligent.

She was honored and recognized as Nashville's

2016 Black 40 under 40 and has been seen on national and international television and heard on several local news and nationally syndicated talk show radio stations such as CBS, NBC, The Word Network, American Family Radio, Total Living Network and more.

SHE'S *Possible*

Find Your Irresistible You

DR. TRILLION SMALL, LMFT

Order *She's Possible* on Amazon

A woman with confidence, clarity, and consistency is unstoppable and simply irresistible. We were born with the ease of touching a heart but somewhere along the line some of us have lost that ability. Not only the ability to captivate other's hearts but the ability to captivate our own heart. Discover and rediscover your irresistible you, today!

Order *The Caged Free Heart* on Amazon

The tug of war between your heart and mind can be one of the greatest battles you will ever have to fight. It is sometimes a fight that leaves us mentally and emotionally bound and metaphorically speaking, incarcerated. But that doesn't have to be how your story ends. If you are searching for mental and emotional freedom this book is for you. This book will help you to:

•Let go of those past pains that are keeping you bound

•Learn how to focus on the present instead of being anxious about tomorrow

•Find the mental and emotional freedom you desire

•Learn how to effectively "re-enter" into the world of relationships without fear and hidden barriers.

True clarity, peace, and freedom awaits you! This is your guide to finding your heart's wings!

INTERNAL NAVIGATOR
BASIC STEPS TO GET YOU FROM POINT A TO POINT B IN YOUR LIFE

2ND EDITION

TRILLION SMALL, PH.D.

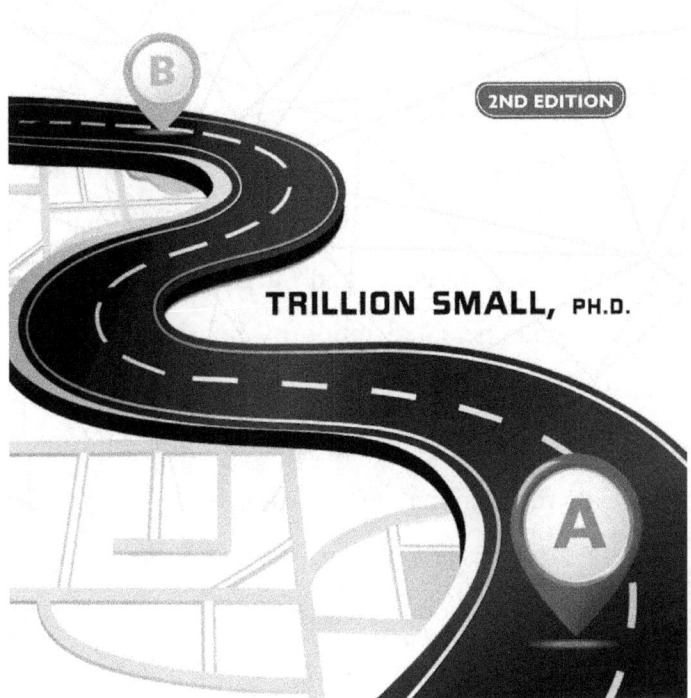

Order *Internal Navigator* on Amazon

A revised edition. In 2013, Internal Navigator began as a guide to discovering and operating fully in your purpose. This second edition expands to include topics of emotional intelligence, psychological hardiness, and mental clutter extraction, to name a few. All in which are much needed on any journey that you embark upon. Just like a navigational system, you have to have a clear understanding of where you currently are and where you desire to go. Getting from Point A to Point B isn't the problem; it's what happens in between both points that can lead to stress, confusion, and fatigue. This book will serve as your personal guide by helping you know what to expect and how to prepare for your unique journey up ahead. Whether you are embarking on a personal, professional, or relationship journey, this book is for you. The scenario may be the same but the principles remain the same.

CONTINUE THE DISCUSSION

Visit my website to book me to speak.

Sign up for my newsletter on my website.

Website: www.trillionsmall.com

Instagram: https://www.instagram.com/trillionsmall

Facebook: https://www.facebook.com/TrillionSmall

Twitter: https://twitter.com/trillionsmall

Youtube: https://www.youtube.com/trillionsmall

TEDxFrisco: www.TEDxFriscotx.com

Purchase the book from my website if you would like a personally autographed copy.

THEY SPEAK PUBLISHING

WWW.THEYSPEAKPUBLISHING.COM

www.ingramcontent.com/pod-product-compliance
Lightning Source LLC
Chambersburg PA
CBHW050213230526
45470CB00001B/357